1995

Divided We Stand

Divided We Stand

Redefining Politics, Technology and Social Choice

Michiel Schwarz

and

Michael Thompson

uɲɲ

University of Pennsylvania Press

Philadelphia

First published in the United States 1990 by
University of Pennsylvania Press
418 Service Drive, Philadelphia
Pennsylvania 19104–6097

Printed and bound in Great Britain.

Library of Congress Cataloging-in-Publication Data

Schwarz, Michiel.
  Divided we stand: redefining politics, technology, and social
choice / Michiel Schwarz and Michael Thompson
      p. cm.
  Includes bibliographical references.
  ISBN 0–8122–8233–7. — ISBN 0–8122–1319–x (pbk).
    1. Environmental policy.   2. Science and state.   3. Technology and
state. I. Thompson, Michael.
HC79.E5S296 1990
302'. 13—dc20   89-38205
                                                                       CIP

302.13
S399

Contents

154, 177

Acknowledgements

Financial support for some of the research reported in this study has been provided by the Science and Engineering Research Council (United Kingdom), the Spencer Foundation (United States), the Science Policy Directorate, Ministry of Education and Sciences (The Netherlands) and the Netherlands Organization for Technology Assessment. Their contributions and assistance are gratefully acknowledged.

Parts of Chapters 7 and 8 have been published in the form of a postscript to Jennifer Brown (ed) *Environmental Threats: Perception, Analysis and Management* (London and New York: Belhaven, 1989). An early version of Chapter 4 appeared in Manfred Grauer, Michael Thompson and Andrej P. Wierzbicki (ed) *Plural Rationality and Interactive Decision Processes*, Lecture Notes in Economics and Mathematical Systems No. 248 (Berlin: Springer, 1985).

We have been fortunate in having readers whose critical comments have challenged us. We thank Aaron Wildavsky and Steve Rayner. Our particular thanks go to Peter James who is in large part the author of the second half of Chapter 6. Responsibility for the context in which his contribution is placed rests, of course, with us.

Because of our focus on matters technological, there are many aspects of the theory we are using (cultural theory, as it is called) that are not developed as far as they could (or should) be. For this reason it may be helpful to read this book as just one part of a trilogy that is completed by a study of leadership by Richard Ellis and Aaron Wildavsky, *Dilemmas of Presidential Leadership* (New Brunswick and Oxford: Transaction, 1989) and an exposition of the foundations of cultural theory by Michael Thompson, Aaron Wildavsky and Richard Ellis, *Cultural Theory* (Boulder, CO: Westview Press, 1990).

Chapter 1

Recognizing and Analyzing the Inchoate

This is an immensely ambitious book. Our aim is to drive a coach and horses through current understandings of the nature of politics, technology and social choice. Politics, we argue, is about much more than the contention of interests. How, we ask, do people who act in their interests come to know where the interests they act in lie? Technology, we argue, is not some exogenous force – perhaps benign, perhaps threatening – that then has impacts on society. Rather, we and it are all caught up together in a social process that is extraordinarily inaccessible to us precisely because we are so much a part of it. And social choice (the aggregation of disparate values) is, we argue, nothing to do with the innate autonomy of the individual and the compromises he then must make in entering into the social contract. To have values, to know what you want, is to already be a social being: an institutionalized individual. We are all 'involved in Mankinde'; the aggregation problem arises not from our becoming involved, but from the different, and often contradictory, ways in which we are already involved.

Our view of politics, technology and social choice is one in which their clear separation is impossible. They are, rather, an entanglement: an inchoate mass. And, if inchoateness is the very essence of politics, technology and social choice, then to try to get to grips with them by making each of them choate (which, we will show, is what current approaches set out to do) is inevitably to distance yourself from them. So we begin, not by getting rid of the inchoate, but by analyzing it. Politics, technology and social choice, we observe, are all entangled because they all hinge crucially upon cognition: upon seeing *and* knowing.

Psycho-physiological entities (John Donne's 'Islands') can certainly see, but only social beings – those who are 'a part of the continent; a peece of the maine' – can know as well. Knowing requires others, and it requires enduring relations with others. Only then can shared patterns of meaning and mutually consistent values, without which knowing is impossible, come into existence. Knowing, in other words, presupposes culture.

So 'cultural theory' by which we mean a synthesis of a number of recent intellectual developments, notably in anthropology and natural resource ecology, is the means by which we seek to achieve our aim. Cultural theory itself is surprisingly simple; the difficulties arise, not in understanding it, but in accepting it and in grasping its import for the conceptions of politics, technology and social choice to which we have long been accustomed. Indeed, the very idea of a *theory* of culture is perhaps the main obstacle to the easy assimilation of our argument. Culture, in the conventional sense of some deadweight of habits and beliefs that is passed on unchanged from generation to generation, tends to be seen as a residual category, an explanation of last resort that is dragged in only when economic, political and organizational explanations have visibly failed to account for what is going on. But if, on confronting the inchoate, we elect not to erase it but to analyze it, then culture – the locus of all the entanglement – can no longer be residual to our theories of politics, technology and social choice. Culture, rather, becomes the essence, the universal solvent through which politics, technology and social choice are all dissolved into one another. A *theory* of culture, therefore, is the first essential. Without that we can have no explicit understanding of all these vital and vexed things that are so much a part of each of us and of our life together.

A little story (a true story) may help us, first, to explain what we mean by the inchoate nature of politics, technology and social choice and, second, to set out the essentials of the cultural theory by which this entanglement can be recognized and analyzed.

The Rim-Blocks Story

A multinational household products corporation recently marketed a lavatory rim-block. They used a waxy material, paradichloroben-zene, to form the active ingredients (perfumes and detergents) into a solid block that would gradually dissolve as the lavatory was flushed. The result sold like hot cakes (indeed, a child actually ate one, but that's another story), and the initial launch in the Netherlands was quickly followed by West Germany, pushing annual production from a few million blocks to more than 30 million. Then, out of the blue, came the bombshell. The German Greens attacked the product, on the grounds that paradichlorobenzene is toxic and non-biodegradable and, therefore, should not be introduced to the water cycle. The firm was convinced that the product was innocuous but, concerned for its reputation in such an environmentally conscious nation, withdrew it from the market and began an urgent search for alternatives.

Within three months there was a replacement product: one which not only eliminated the offending paradichlorobenzene but also had the major advantages of a better smell, lower evaporation in store, and production by continuous extrusion instead of the previous batch-moulding technique. The corporation's newsletter put it like this:

> The result was actually a better product in terms of perfume delivery and product life – a less expensive product and a new process with higher production capability. Armed with this the German launch went from strength to strength. We are now allowing the UK housewife to enjoy some of the benefits of our research efforts.

All that was missing from this piece of self-congratulation was the corporation's heartfelt thanks to the German Greens!

So here is our problem. How was it that, despite the long deliberation and intensive market research that precedes any new product launch, and despite previous conflict with environmental groups in Germany and in other countries, our multinational was still *surprised* by the Greens' response? Most observers would surely identify that movement as one of the most salient influences on any company distributing enormous quantities of those dread products, chemicals, for that dubious purpose, profit, to that sacred repository of motherhood and apple-pie, the home. So why, with all the scientific, marketing, environmental and managerial expertise at its disposal, did it take a prod from a few Greens to reveal the 'better mousetrap' that all the time was latent in the company's resources?

Our answer is: conflicting perceptions of the natural environment – *contradictory certainties*. The Greens see nature as vulnerable to human abuse; they place the burden of proof on those who want to innovate. Because paradichlorobenzene has never been directly introduced to the water cycle before, and because the precious resource of clean water[1] is already under threat, the slightest doubt as to its toxicity or biodegradability should require its removal from the market. Our multinational, of course, wants to protect the environment but perceives nature to be more robust than do the Greens: it places the burden of proof on the objectors. Provided proper precautions are taken, such as OECD toxicity testing, it is reasonable to introduce new materials into the ecosystem.

There are three things we wish to make clear about such contradictory views of nature:

1. they are not uncommon;
2. they lie beyond the reach of both orthodox ('what are the facts?') scientific method and the conventional notion of 'decision making under uncertainty'; and
3. their study brings natural and social scientists together in a new and interesting way.

These three assertions provide the basis for our entire argument. They also, in a rather back-to-front way, provide the structure for our book. In the chapters that follow we will gradually and, we hope, persuasively substantiate our first two assertions: the prevalence of the inchoate and its inaccessibility from current approaches. Here, by rushing ahead to our third assertion, we will give an informal outline of the 'new synthesis' that allows access to the inchoate and then use it to resolve the problem we have set ourselves: why the multinational was surprised.

The Natural Science

Ecologists who study *managed* ecosystems, such as forests, fisheries and grasslands, encounter the managing institutions as sets of interventions in those systems. Time and time again they have found that different managing institutions, faced with exactly the same kinds of situation, adopt strategies based on one of four different interpretations of ecosystem stability (Holling 1979, 1986, Timmerman 1986). These four 'myths of nature' as they call them – each of which, the ecologists insist, captures *some* essence of experience and wisdom – can be graphically represented by a ball in a landscape (Figure 1.1).

Nature benign gives us global equilibrium. Such a world is

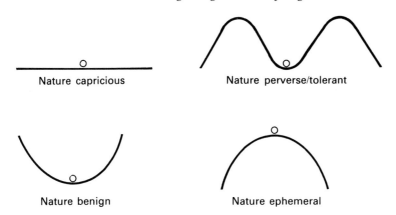

Figure 1.1 The myths of nature.

wonderfully forgiving: no matter what knocks we deliver the ball will always return to the bottom of the basin. The managing institutions can therefore have a *laissez-faire* attitude. *Nature ephemeral* is almost the exact opposite. The world, it tells us, is a terribly unforgiving place and the least jolt may cause its catastrophic collapse. The managing institutions must treat the ecosystem with great care. This is the view of the German Greens. *Nature perverse/ tolerant*, though it may look like a cross between the first two, is quite different. Its world is one that is forgiving of most events, but is vulnerable to an occasional knocking of the ball over the rim. The managing institutions must therefore regulate against unusual occurrences. Our multinational is to be found here. It accepts that the small risk of disaster necessitates government regulation, but believes that, once minimum standards have been met, it should be free to make its own decisions. Finally, *nature capricious* is a random world; institutions with this view of nature do not really manage, nor do they learn. They just cope with erratic events.

Each of these views of nature appears irrational from the perspective of any other. For the Greens, the multinational is irrational because it fails to see that paradichlorobenzene could be the final insult that sends the ball rolling down the slope. For the multinational, the Greens' failure to recognize that nature is relatively stable creates an irrational concern with 'obviously' minor risks, like paradichlorobenzene, and a neglect of apparently more serious ones, such as smoking or car-driving. As a result, society is deprived of the benefits of innovation.

Another way of putting it is that each actor is perfectly rational, given his or her convictions as to how the world is. The situation is one of *plural rationality*, and the question it prompts us to ask is: how is each actor given his or her convictions? This brings us to the social science.

The Social Science

The four myths of nature identified by ecologists map onto the typology of social relationships that has been developed by the anthropologist Mary Douglas and her co-workers (Douglas 1978, 1982, Thompson 1983a,b, Gross and Rayner 1985). This typology is based on the answers to two central and eternal questions of human existence: 'who am I?' and 'how should I behave?' Personal identity, it is argued, is determined by individuals' relationships to *groups*. Those who belong to a strong group – a collective that makes decisions binding on all members – will see themselves very differently to those who have weak ties with others and therefore make choices that bind only themselves. Behaviour is shaped by the extent of the social prescriptions (the *grid* dimension) that an individual is subject to: a spectrum which runs from the free spirit to the tightly constrained. These two 'dimensions of sociality', as they are called, generate four basic, and stabilizable, forms of social relationship. And, in each instance, just one of the plural rationalities can *do* the stabilizing (Figure 1.2).

Two of these 'archetypes' – individualists and hierarchists – are already familiar to social scientists. Indeed, the sociologist Max Weber (1958), the political scientist Charles Lindblom (1977) and the institutional economist Oliver Williamson (1975), are only three of the scholars who have based entire bodies of theory on this distinction between *markets* and *hierarchies*, and the accompanying observation that each promotes a distinctive form of rationality that legitimizes and enables its operation. Market cultures stress the autonomy of individuals and their resulting freedom to bid and bargain with each other: they have a *substantive rationality*. The 'bottom line' is what they care for, not the relational niceties of the people who happen to have come together to achieve that result. Hierarchies are made up of bounded social groups, each of which is in an orderly and ranked relationship with each other. Their attempts to coordinate these components, without violating status

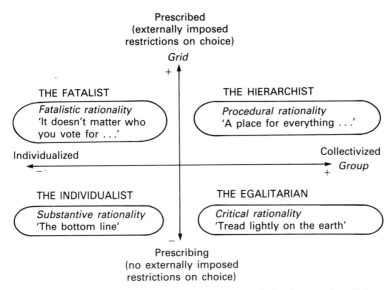

Figure 1.2 The two dimensions of sociality and the four rationalities.

differentials, creates a *procedural rationality* that is more concerned with the proprieties of who does what than with trying to evaluate the outcome (if there is one).

But this is an inadequate taxonomy. Many people reject both the individualism of the market and the inequalities of the hierarchy: they prefer the *egalitarian groups* of our diagram. They have a communal and *critical rationality*, which stresses the importance of fraternal and sororal cooperation, and therefore strives for social relationships that are voluntaristic and egalitarian. But, since this desired state of affairs is always threatened by the encroachment of hierarchy (which brings status differences) or by excessive individualism (which all too easily introduces inequalities of wealth, power and knowledge), collective identity has all the time to be sustained by a shared and strident criticism of what goes on outside the group. Historically, this rationality has been the driving force of socialism (but, as that movement has grown, it has been increasingly diluted by hierarchy and political entrepreneurialism) and today it is alive and well as the preferred organizational form of the Greens (and of many single-issue public interest groups in the United States).

It is also a cruel travesty to describe all those who are individualized as bustling and untrammelled entrepreneurs: as paid-up members of 'the enterprise culture'. Many have so many prescriptions on their behaviour that they have minimal freedom of choice: for example, the unemployed, trailing from one welfare centre to another *ad infinitum*. These are the marginal members of society – *the fatalists* – whose inability to influence events this way or that engenders a *fatalistic rationality* in which outcomes, good or bad, are simply to be enjoyed or endured, but never achieved.

Each of these rationalities, when acted upon, both sustains and justifies the particular organizational form that goes along with it. The high-rise, system-built tower block, for instance, is the hierarchist's solution to the housing problem; gentrification, the individualist's; cooperative self-build, the egalitarian's; homelessness, the fatalist's. Hierarchists trim and prune social transactions until they fit neatly into their orderly ambit, individualists pull them into the marketplace, egalitarians strive to capture them into a kind of voluntary minimalism (which, to those on the outside, often looks more like 'coercive utopianism'), and fatalists endure with more or less dignity whatever comes their way.

We can now see how each of the myths of nature (the ecologist's explanation for 'managerial heterogeneity') legitimates and reproduces certain kinds of institutional relationships (the anthropologist's cultural categories) (Figure 1.3).

This diagram, of course, is just the two earlier ones – the ecologist's and the anthropologist's – combined, and to back-track for a moment, this is what we meant about the study of contradictory certainties bringing natural and social scientists together in a new and interesting way.

The New Synthesis

The world of nature benign is most hospitable to individualists. As long as we all do our individualistic, exuberant things, a 'hidden hand' (the uniformly downward slope of the landscape) will lead us to the best possible outcome. Since restrictions on individual freedom, and therefore on experimentation, would impede the attainment of this outcome, the myth of a benign nature furnishes a powerful moral justification for these particular modes of acting and learning. If we take, for example, the topical issue of hazardous waste management, nature benign would indicate that a sharpening of market incentives (transferable 'rights to pollute', brokers to

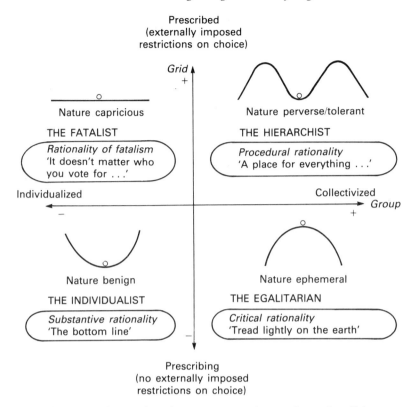

Figure 1.3 The myths of nature mapped onto the rationalities.

reduce the transaction and information costs of connecting some firms' waste streams into other firms' feedstocks, self-policing to increase consumer confidence, etc.) is the way to go.

By contrast, an ephemeral nature suits egalitarian groups very well. Their small-scale organizations tread lightly upon our fragile earth, and they are only too happy to re-educate those who, in persisting in stamping around wildly, threaten the destruction of the entire planet. Minimal perturbation becomes the overriding moral imperative, and small becomes beautiful. Trials can go ahead only if it is certain there will be no errors. By these criteria many of the products of our consumer society are not just unnecessary, they are actually destroying the one earth that should be our most sacred trust. The myth of nature ephemeral tells us that there will have to be radical change *now*, before it is too late. Since most hazardous wastes are discharged into the environment from the production systems that, directly or indirectly, give us all these products (rimblocks, for instance) that we do not need and should not have, the solution is an outright ban (or, better still, a consumer rejection) on all unnecessary products: a solution that has the added advantage of bringing us much nearer to the desired future – harmony with nature.

Nature perverse/tolerant requires strong social controls to ensure that the ball never crosses the rim. And to apply those controls effectively you need precise knowledge of the line between equilibrium and disequilibrium. Neither the unbridled experimentation that goes with the zone of equilibrium, nor the timorous forbearance that accompanies the zone of disequilibrium can command much moral authority here. Rather, everything hinges upon mapping and managing the boundary line that separates these zones. Complete knowledge, certainty and predictability, generated by and for those whose pre-eminent task is to keep each mode of action – social sanctions and individual experiments – in its proper place, becomes the dominant moral concern. The situation cries out for hierarchy: sober, expert and, above all, enduring. Only then can we have an orderly solution matched to the time scales and complexities of the problem: standard-setting, cradle-to-grave materials accounting systems, trip tickets, site licences, spot checks and precisely detailed lists of hazardous wastes.

Nature capricious is the natural habitat for those with neither standing nor influence in society. In the other three rationalities, learning is possible (though each is disposed to learn different things) but in the flatland of nature capricious there are no gradients to teach us the differences between hills and dales, up and down, better and worse. Life is, and remains, a lottery. The world does things to you while you do nothing to it. All you can do is try to cope, as best you can, with a situation over which you have no control. Though those who find themselves attached to this myth produce no policies for the management of hazardous wastes, they are by no means irrelevant to those policies that are produced. They are the great risk absorbers, enduring with more or less dignity, greater or lesser ignorance, whatever comes their way: a social sponge that the active policy makers, in their different ways, publicly wring their hands over and privately make good use of. Without the passive risk absorbers (and the contradictory claims that are always made on their behalf), the rest of us would not be able to get any of our preferred policies to work.

It is by teasing out these rationalities that we can begin to make sense of what is going on in all those policy debates that are characterized by contradictory certainties. Though this approach *is* saying that knowledge is socially constructed, it is *not* saying that the world can be any way we want it to be. It is *not* saying that we can know nothing; only that we cannot know everything and that, within that uncertain and inchoate region, it is our institutions – our social involvements – that lead us to grant credibility to one possible state of affairs rather than another.

There are a great many predictions that follow from this 'new synthesis', but the most useful for our present purposes is that each rationality will generate its own distinctive engineering aesthetic: its own definition of the good, the beautiful and the socially desirable.

Modern hierarchies are biased towards large-scale, high-technology approaches that demand much specialized knowledge and centralized direction. The egalitarians' distaste for these requirements drives them towards small-scale, environmentally benign technology (usually low-tech, but using microelectronics when this saves energy and reduces pollution). For many years their watchword has been 'appropriate technology' but in reality this is the motto of the individualists: it is they who are happy to operate at any size, to any technical specification, within their capabilities, providing it is cheap enough to make them a profit and cheerful enough to attract the punters.

Returning now to the lavatory rim-blocks, we can observe that large corporations face outwardly towards markets but, within themselves, tend to be strongly hierarchical. Their normal manner of progress is towards ever more specialized products, using ever more specialized processes and materials, and ultimately creating ever greater organizational differentiation and complexity. Their primary focus is the internal technology/skills package rather than the customer (the individualists' primary focus) or the human race and its biosphere (the egalitarians' primary focus). Nothing more natural, then, for a multinational to utilize a high-tech material such as paradichlorobenzene (and the moulding technology which goes with it) in one area of its business and then to extend it to others.

But the egalitarian engineering aesthetic is suspicious of lavatory rim-blocks. Are they, like deodorants, a corporate appropriation of hygiene: a conspiracy aimed at convincing us that what is natural is nasty: original sin slickly harnessed to company profits? But, since this critical aesthetic does not (and probably could not) exist within the company, it is initially manifested as *the enemy*, an homogeneous green *other* that threatens not only the company's business but also the entire way of life of its members and of its contented customers.

The individualists are less doctrinally committed. Being pragmatic materialists, they will try to align themselves with whichever development path offers them the best financial prospects. They do exist within our multinational, awaiting, like resting actors, the call of the venture capitalist. They see that the corporation is losing its battle and needs to withdraw; they slowly persuade the startled hierarchy to transfer the Greens from the category of 'alien other' to the more comprehensible one of 'dissatisfied customer'. They do this, not because they have suddenly gone over to vegetarianism and nuclear freezes, but because they know a miserable customer (and eventually) a more profitable product when they see one.

However (and this is the crux of our whole argument), neither the hierarchical nor the individualistic rationality could actually *see* the better product, and switch over to it, until the Greens' rude intrusion forced the non-incremental jump from one development path to another. Without this external pressure, the multinational's obvious capacity to better satisfy each of these aesthetics (for the new high-tech, profitable and environmentally more acceptable product could not otherwise have been developed so quickly) would have remained undeveloped.

The simple but profound message is that the cultural pluralism is *essential*. The three active rationalities – the hierarchical, the individualistic and the egalitarian – structure the world in different and (in the right circumstances) complementary ways.[2] And, lest it appear that, as usual, they have been missed out, we should stress that the fatalists too are essential (in their passive way), because each of the active rationalities seeks to advance its cause by mobilizing them. 'Just get the hierarchists and the egalitarians off their backs', say the individualists, 'and they'll soon lift themselves up by their own bootstraps'. 'Once the inequitable markets and hierarchies have been eliminated', the egalitarians argue, 'there will be no one to poison or otherwise oppress you. Only when we are all meek will we at last inherit our fragile earth'. The hierarchists, pointing to their code of *noblesse oblige*, and to the idea of a ruler being responsive to the (suitably modest) needs of the ruled, argue for the fatalists getting a better deal in the hierarchy than they would in the free-for-all of the marketplace or in the egalitarian millennium (if it ever comes).

By directing our attention to the social influences on cognition, and to the plural rationalities they sustain, this new synthesis tells us that it is our institutions which analyze the inchoate. It is our institutions that are the repositories of our myths: the structures which frame individual awareness (Douglas 1986). And it is in the play of our institutions that wisdom lies, for, as each rationality adapts to the others, so a kind of meta-understanding of the inchoate is generated. Our concern, therefore, should not be with which one is *right* (for that would be to insist that just one rationality had access to 'the truth') but rather with which is *appropriate* to the task at hand. There is no final solution; there is no rationality without its institutional context; there is no complete knowledge. Diversity, contradiction, contention and criticism (the basic ingredients of this 'new synthesis') are the best tools we have for understanding the inchoate. We must learn to husband them and make the most of them. Divided we stand; united we fall.

Notes

1. As opposed to *cleaned* water: something which, since it differs markedly from the water that for millions of years has been so vital a part of the environment in which we have evolved, is viewed with grave suspicion (Davis 1987).

2. The ecologist C.S. Holling has captured this complementarity by a meta-myth: nature resilient. Nature resilient focuses on the transformational properties of ball and landscape – the way the movement of the ball actually changes the shape of the landscape through which it moves – and in so doing subsumes the four primary myths as phases within an ever-repeating cycle of transformation.

Chapter 2

What's Special About Technological Decision Making?

Our rim-block story has taken us right into a topical piece of technological development. The established technology was progressing, on automatic pilot as it were, along the hierarchists' chosen trajectory until it was so rudely and so unexpectedly interrupted by the Greens. When the dust had finally settled the technology was no longer on its old trajectory (Dosi 1982). The Greens' broadside and the individualists' crash programme, together, had set it on a quite different and (by all their varied criteria) much better path. Decisions – momentous decisions that suddenly and dramatically changed the course of technological development – had been made. Of that there can be no doubt, but who *made* those decisions?

The Greens certainly did not. All they did was to stop things going the way they were. The hierarchists did not. All they did was instigate the crash programme and give the okay to the new product that it came up with. The individualists did not. All they did was seize the opportunity that the others presented them with. None of them, we must conclude, made the decision. The decision was, somehow, made between them. Yet even this strange answer will not do. The word 'between' suggests that they all got together and thrashed out the decision in a spirit of constructive compromise, and this they certainly did not do. No, it would be nearer the truth to say that the decision was made, not between them, but in spite of them! (Nor should we overlook nature's role in all this. Though there is disagreement over whether the paradichlorobenzene does any harm or not, there is no doubt that it does find its way into the water cycle and, moving to the other end of the rim-block's life, no matter whether you are a hierarchical, an individualistic or an

14

egalitarian production engineer you cannot continuously extrude the waxy material from which it is formed. Though we may like to think that it is we who press the button on the environment, the environment can also press the button on us. Often enough, as with the rim-blocks, it is a bit of both.)

The rim-block's remarkable change of technological direction, we can say, is a textbook example of inter-institutional decision making. Or, rather, it would be if such examples were given in any of the textbooks. Unfortunately, the textbooks do not allow for this sort of thing. The rim-block story tells us that it was the system (and, in particular, the contradictory certainties embedded in the system) that made the decision. It was the fundamental contradiction of its parts that shifted the whole onto its new trajectory (and it was nature that ultimately made those trajectories both possible and different). This, in a nutshell, is our view of technological decision making, and it is a view that does not readily align itself with the conventional wisdom. The conventional wisdom can be characterized by three founding assumptions:

1. that technological decision making is different from other kinds of decision making because, unlike them, it has a *substantive* technical core;
2. that disputes over technological choices centre not on the technology itself (for that, being substantive, is indisputable), but on the *impacts* it is likely to have on society; and
3. that, when technical uncertainties allow facts and values to become entwined (as happens, for instance, when experts disagree), that entwinement is not inherent to the technology but is derived from the *pre-existing* political persuasions of those involved.

These three assumptions deny our starting point: the inchoateness of politics, technology and social choice. To say that technology, above and beyond its admitted involvement in politics and personal preferences, always retains a substantive core is to say that, to a considerable and indisputable extent, it stands by itself. To say that this free-standing core then has impacts *on* something outside itself – society – is to say that it is possible, in principle, to identify those impacts, to assess them in terms of their costs and benefits to the various parts within the social whole (these parts revealing themselves by their self-evident interests), and to then perform some sort of juggling exercise that by maximizing the benefits and minimizing the costs will enable us to arrive at the best social choice.[1] And to say that, outside of this substantive technical core, the entwinement of facts and values is brought about by the pre-existing political orientations of those involved is to say that the contending interests of those involved have a self-sustaining existence above and beyond the fray into which, from time to time, they descend.

This chapter, and the two that follow it, set out this conventional wisdom, as expressed in these three founding assumptions, and show how it signally fails to make contact with the phenomena with which it claims to be dealing.

Controversies in Technological Decision Making

Despite the conceptual difficulties in separating technological decisions from other controversial policy concerns, analysts have consistently treated disputes over science and technology as being in a class of their own – a class with its own distinctive label: 'technological decision making'. The justification for this, as Dorothy Nelkin has made clear, is the substantive (and largely beneficial) core – the technology itself – which then has some rather uneven social impacts.

> Technologies of speed and power – airports, electric power utilities, highways, dams – provoke bitter political antagonism as local communities protest against increasing burdens of noise, pollution and disruption. Great technological advances are invariably controversial; along with their benefits they generate distressing side effects (Nelkin 1974a: 1).

The special status that is thus attributed to technology as a source of political conflict, pervades the literature on controversial technological decisions. Empirical studies regularly take the political debate about the potential 'side effects' of a technological development as their starting point, thereby identifying their subject of concern in relation to the substantive issues of science and technology (Lawless 1977, Hetman 1973, OECD 1978, Dierkes *et al.* 1980, Hohenemser and Kasperson 1982).

> Whatever political values motivate controversy, the debates usually focus on technical questions. The siting controversies (for example) develop out of concern with the quality of life in a community,

but the debates revolve around technical questions – the physical requirements for the facility, the accuracy of the predictions establishing its need, or the precise extent of environmental risk (Nelkin 1979: 16).

Before accepting this characterization of the policy debate that accompanies technological decision making we should pause to consider the character of policy debates in general.

All policy debates revolve around *people* and *ideas*. Poverty, for instance, has to do with some people's lack of command over resources relative to their needs, and poverty policy has to do with the ideas of distributional justice that define a more desirable state of affairs (the policy goal) and with the ideas both of the processes by which poverty comes about and of the ways we can intervene in those processes to modify their outcomes (the instrumental means towards the policy goal). But some policy debates, the conventional wisdom tells us, revolve around *things* as well (nuclear power stations, double helixes, motorway boxes, word processors, liquefied natural gas terminals, Channel tunnels, and so on), and it is this quality of 'thingness' that has been used to separate out technological decision making as a distinct kind of decision making, one in which the debate revolves around a technical and factual core that simply does not exist in other kinds of decision making.

It is with this starting point that we take issue. There is, we insist, no policy debate that is devoid of things, though, of course, some are more thing-ridden than others. Poverty policy, for instance, is not usually considered a part of technological decision making yet, as the 'office proletariat' implications of information technology (to give a topical example) make clear, it is nevertheless much involved with things as well as with people and ideas. Nor are the facts concerning those things, and the uncertainties that often surround those facts, ever merely technical. They are every bit as value-driven as are any of the other interactions within this triangular interplay of people, ideas and things. Where others have assumed the interplay of just people and ideas to be the natural habitat of policy, and have then had to designate a special category of decision making for those environments where things are involved as well, we begin by assuming that this 'special case' is the normal (indeed, the inescapable) state of affairs, and then set out to explore the continuum of variation in policy debates as the relative contributions of these three essential elements – people, ideas and things – vary.

Given the ambitious and contentious nature of our claim, we must begin by establishing that the position we are attacking is indeed garrisoned by the ranks of the orthodox. A revolution that got us to where we already were by insisting that actually we were somewhere else would be no revolution at all! Accordingly, this and the next chapter are concerned simply to demonstrate that this is not what we are doing: that the definers of technological decision making are very far from being straw men and women.

The Orthodox Garrison and its Conceptual Citadel

In singling out policy problems related to science and technology, analysts have tried to discern the distinctive empirical features that have characterized controversial cases of technological decision making in the past (OECD 1979, Hetman 1973, Wenk 1984, Porter *et al.* 1982, Coates and Fabian 1982, Umweltbundesamt 1983). An Organisation for Economic Co-operation and Development study group, for example, identified a cluster of six main factors. These included the novelty and complexity of the issues associated with scientific and technological developments, the dimensions of their impacts, the ethical and value concerns, and the perceptions of the general public (OECD 1979). Essentially, all these factors are concerned with how the *impacts* of science and technology (on health, on the environment, on ethical principles, and so on) should be assessed and evaluated. In similar vein, the disparate views on the assessment of the risks and benefits associated with technological projects or developments have been seen as dictating the emergence and outcome of disputes (Nelkin 1983, Dierkes *et al.* 1980. Conrad 1980). The common assumption has been that science and technology, for all its admitted uncertainties, is *factual*, and that *values* come into play only in relation to the impacts that this substantive core then has upon society.

Given this initial orientation, the analysis of controversial techno-logical decisions has been concerned with conflicting assessments of technology; with trying to account for differences among policy actors in identifying and evaluating potential impacts. The early literature on technology assessment (TA) has viewed policy contro-versies over the risks and benefits of a technology as involving two distinct areas of potential dissensus: scientific disagreement among technical experts, and value conflicts as to the social and political evaluation of the technology's impacts (Roessner and Frey 1974,

Lowrance 1976). However, as technology assessments have increasingly entered the political arena, and as some of the technologies have become subject to considerable public controversy, it has become apparent that this separation of factual impacts and political evaluations is highly problematic. Technology assessment is, to use an overworked phrase, in crisis. It has set out by insisting that technology and society are separate and has then found them to be inextricably entwined.

Our argument begins by rejecting the conventional starting point: the neat separation of technical facts and social values. Anthropologists and sociologists of knowledge have shown us that what are considered facts depends ultimately on an accepted framework of social (and therefore evaluative) premises. Even scientific knowledge, whilst not perhaps wholly fluid, is certainly plastic in the sense that it is socially negotiated (science being a social activity) and moulded by values of various kinds. (Barnes 1974, Mulkay 1979, Law and French 1974, Knorr-Cetina and Mulkay 1983, Douglas 1975, Barnes and Edge 1982). However, our main concern here, whilst consistent with and informed by this social constructivist view (summarized in Campbell 1982, Berger and Luckmann 1967), is more with the policy-analytic implications of the entwinement of facts and values.

Essentially, we are rejecting the single-framework assumption that goes with the clear separability of facts and values. Instead, we see that as just one of several contending frameworks each of which defines 'the problem' in a different way, and each of which generates its own assessment of a technology in terms of its own definition of what that technology is (Wynne 1974, Berg 1975).

Our solution to the crisis of technology assessment is achieved, first, by taking on board the relativist implications of the social constructivist school and, second, by teasing out the constraints – both physical and social – that set some bounds on the proliferation of socially constructed technologies. Such accepted frameworks, we will show, are multiple but not infinite. And, since they are inevitably in contention with one another, technology can never be some factual core aloof from the valuational debate over its impacts. Rather, technology is a social process. It is part and parcel of a political fray, one important component of which is the current attempt to insist that it is above it.

The separation of facts and values and the birth of Nimbies and Lulus

Much of the empirical literature on controversial technological decisions can be challenged on its implicit assumption that 'consequences' are identifiable separately from 'value' concerns. Case studies of facility siting disputes (often involving large-scale technologies) have been particularly active in promoting the idea that policy dissensus stems simply from conflicting evaluations of 'the' technological risks and benefits. In this view, the risks and benefits associated with a technology are not in themselves considered problematic in policy disputes. Problems are seen as arising only in the sense that policy actors reveal conflicting preferences on their desirability.

This interpretation does not attribute controversy to 'factual' disputes over what the risks and benefits *are*, but only to the distribution of these impacts (Brooks 1984). It focuses on 'objective' differences among policy actors to account for the fact that technologies may affect various groups in society in different ways (Nelkin 1977: 431, La Porte 1975). Disparities between national and local interests, between general and specific concerns, have typically been identified as underpinning conflicting impact assessments. (O'Hare *et al.* 1983, Morell and Magorian 1982). In facility siting controversies, O'Hare *et al.* (1983:1) have characterized the issue as 'the problem of locally undesirable though generally beneficial' projects, an approach that has now sired that increasingly troublesome child, Lulu (Locally Unwanted Land Use).[2] Similarly, Nelkin stresses the equity issue as central to the emergence of many technological disputes, when she generalizes:

> Many controversies arise when citizens in a community become aware that they must bear the cost of a project that will benefit a different much broader constituency. Airports and power plants serve large regions, but neighbours bear the environmental and social burden (Nelkin 1979: 11).

Such accounts of so-called Nimby (Not In My Back Yard) disputes are conceptually deficient in that they assume (or at least suggest) that technological impacts can be unambiguously defined in their factual dimensions. Like Lulus, this notion of Nimbies assumes that the dispute is simply over where these desirable facilities should be sited and diverts attention away from the frequent existence of policy actors who see those facilities as highly *un*desirable, and whose *global* aim is that they not be sited anywhere. Nor, to make matters worse, can these global actors, when they are present in a dispute, be clearly separated from the Nimbies. It is not uncommon for a policy actor to set off as a Nimby and to become transformed into a Niaby (Not In Anyone's Back Yard) as the policy process develops.

Those pillars of British society – farmers, vicars, school mistresses and local squires – who have in recent years fought off attempts by Nirex (the waste disposal arm of the British nuclear industry) to dispose of low-level radioactive waste in shallow trenches in their localities have, in many instances, expressed their profound dismay at the behaviour of institutions that, until then, they had trusted implicitly. It is through this sort of involvement (involvement that quite often leads them, for the first time in their lives, to deliberately break the law of the land) that local objectors are sometimes transformed into global resistors. Consciousness, alas, does not receive much attention in the conventional wisdom that has given us the Nimby. According to it, people spring to the defence of their self-evident interests, and that is that. The fact that the very act of springing may conjure up interests that simply were not there before, and displace those that were there – something that can so rapidly erode the credibility of long-established institutions, and the sustainability of the technological trajectories those institutions promote – is accorded no place in the analysis.

Of course, we do not claim that consciousness raising and interest transformation are always present; only that their absence cannot be assumed. Studies of controversies over technological impacts confirm that, whilst the absence of conflicts over the identification of risks and benefits may sometimes be an empirical outcome, it cannot be taken as a conceptual premise for analysis. In many health-related controversies (e.g., over the health hazards of low-level radiation, or the effects of certain drugs), the question of determining risks and benefits is at the very centre of the dispute (Mazur 1981, Nelkin 1979, Petersen and Markle 1979, Gillespie *et al.* 1979, Eva and Rothman 1979). Similarly, environmental controversies often manifest themselves in conflicting stances as to what are to be taken as the ecological impacts of technological developments.

What is clear from real-life cases is that policy actors regularly adopt strikingly different notions of the risks and benefits associated with technological developments. Here one only has to refer to the literature on what are called 'perceived risks' to emphasize that conflicting measures of technological impacts must be accepted as part of empirical reality in policy discussions over risk and contro-versial technology (Covello 1983, Brown 1989). Many disputes, moreover, have involved disagreement among scientific experts over the nature and effects of various potential impacts (an issue that is discussed in more detail in Chapter 3). The political analysis of technological decisions must, therefore, be based on the understand-ing that both technological impacts and their social evaluation may be subject to controversy. The substantive core can be, and often is, totally without substance.

Political values and impact assessments

On those occasions when the entwinement of facts and values has been recognized, its implications have been fudged. Many political accounts of technological decision disputes, in acknowledging that facts cannnot be assumed to be value-neutral, have accepted that the identification of risks and benefits inevitably involves evaluative commitments. However, in the dominant perspective of the policy sciences, it is the value stances of the policy actors that are advanced as the central determinants for the identification and assessment of technological impacts. Hence, despite the apparent rejection of a naive separation of factual disputes from political value conflicts, the traditional approach still fails to come to terms with the *structural interdependence* of facts and values in controversies. In trying to account for the contending boundaries that policy actors set to the identification of technological impacts, most studies reflect an instrumental view of the political selection process. They have treated conflicting definitions of technological consequences not as being in themselves problematic, but simply as manifestations of underlying dissensus over social and political values. It is this narrow political conceptualization of technology assessment disputes that we wish to challenge.

Those who study and analyze technological decision disputes have failed to recognize that any demarcation between factual impacts and social value dimensions in technological choice is, in itself, a significant controversial feature that needs to be explained. They have failed to acknowledge that processes of 'impact assessment' are inherently ambiguous and, as such, are always open to political debate. What is considered a technical fact, and what is seen as belonging to the realm of social values, need to be treated as part of the empirical dispute over *definitional* boundaries that is integral to technological decision controversies. What is lacking in most of the literature is the acknowledgement that impact assessments, far from reflecting conflicting evaluations of the facts, involve rival *interpretive frames* in which facts and values are all bound up together.

Some authors, however, have convincingly argued this structural ambiguity in impact assessment. Nowotny, for instance, in the context of the nuclear power controversy, has concluded that

> The societal images of nuclear risk . . . display the same [ambiguous] quality: depending how one looks at them the risks involved are entirely technical in origin as well as in terms of a solution to the problem they contain, or they are entirely social, depending on the functioning or lack of it, of social institutions from the initial planning to the control of safeguards (Nowotny 1977: 243–64).

Here, at last, we see the aloofness of technology treated as just one of the socially accepted frameworks that underlie the political debate and, indeed, actually make that debate possible.

From this perspective, the closure of a controversy must be seen as dependent on consensus on the boundaries to the relevant facts of the case, as well as the appropriate evaluative criteria for choice. The analysis of technological decisions therefore should not, and cannot, be premised on any *a priori* separation between its factual and value dimensions. Indeed, it has been suggested that the dual nature of fact–value disputes is essentially what makes 'trans-scientific' controversies in technological decision making so problematic (Rip 1983, Petersen and Markle 1979, Collingridge 1980, ch. 12, Fischoff *et al.* 1981, Schwarz 1983, Irwin 1985).[3] In short, what is required is not just to acknowledge that facts are value-laden but to adopt an analytical approach that can come to terms with the interaction between factual and value dimensions in a single conceptual frame.

This brings us to the conventional wisdom's third founding assumption: that the entwinement of facts and values in technological debates, when it occurs, is 'imported' from outside – the enforced politicization of something that itself can have no politics.

Notes

1. Students of that esoteric subject, distributive justice, will know that, depending on the principle chosen (Pareto optimal, Golden Rule, Rawlsian, etc), the best social choice will turn out quite differently, which just goes to show that the initial separation of politics, technology and social choice is not valid, and that the outcome based on the assumption that it is valid is never unequivocal. (For a concise survey of this minefield see Schulze 1980).

2. In much the same way, the detailed study of a technological pollution control project in the Delaware River Basin (Ackerman *et al.* 1974) focuses on how different views as to how the costs and benefits should be distributed and identified as the main source of the controversy. In this particular case, the disparate views on the identification and evaluation of impacts were traced back to institutional conflicts of federal versus regional policy actors.

3. We thus go well beyond the notion of 'trans-science' as introduced by Weinberg (1972): trans-scientific questions not only transcend science when it comes to their resolution, but involve fundamental issues on the extent that scientific facts and social values can be separated.

Chapter 3

Disputes among Experts (And among Experts on Disputes among Experts)

'Nuclear power? No thanks!' reads one car-sticker; 'Stone Age? No thanks!' reads another. Each car owner knows, with certainty, what the other denies; neither can opt out of the future that the other is so anxious to bestow on him. 'Whose, if anyone's, future wins?' is the big question, a question in which politics, technology and social choice are all tangled up together, along with profoundly contradictory convictions both as to what the facts at issue are and as to what sort of a society (small-scale and decentralized or large-scale and centralized, for instance) is to be striven for.

The conventional response – scientific research to determine what the facts at issue really are – has met its match (for the moment, at least) in this sort of polarized policy debate. And, even when the facts *can* be established, many important decisions will have been made in the interim. Nor, for all the trouble they are now causing, is there anything particularly new or untypical about these inchoate entwinements of facts and values. Almost all the technologies we now live with (the cars to which we fix our divergent stickers, for instance) went through their crucial early stages in a cloud of contradictory certainties. (Arthur 1985). The challenge, therefore, is not to deny this cloud but to understand it.

Perhaps the best indicator of the cloud's presence is the persistent disagreement among experts. All of us, and not just the analysts of technological politics, are now accustomed to seeing experts disagreeing (almost nightly on television) over just about everything technological – from lavatory rim-blocks to fast-breeder reactors, from aerosol sprays to genetic engineering, from the health effects of fertilizer residues to the codisposal of toxic and domestic waste

in landfill sites. What is more, we are used to them going on and on disagreeing. They will never agree, we realize, because, like the two women that Sidney Smith saw shouting at each other from their houses on opposite sides of an Edinburgh street, they are arguing from different premises. It is, therefore, the different premises – the contradictory certainties and their institutional origins – that are the key to understanding the cloud itself.

But those who have set out by insisting that technological decision making, by virtue of its substantive core, is in a class of its own cannot concede that the premises are different. To do that would be to deny the existence of the substantive core. And that substantive core, as we have already seen, is what justifies their treating technological decision making as a distinct kind of decision making. They have, therefore, to follow a different line of reasoning; one that leaves the core (and, therefore, their unique area of expertise) intact. Their argument goes something like this: since expert disagreements over factual and scientific evidence (over the substantive core, that is) are now becoming accepted features of many technological decision controversies (Benveniste 1972, Schooler 1971, Nelkin 1974b, 1975, Nichols 1979, Frankena 1983), there is clearly a need for a theory of decision making that can accommodate the fact that experts are likely to disagree (Collingridge 1980: 191).

The conventional mode of political analysis – the politics of interest, as we shall be calling it – neatly satisfies this need. The pre-existing value conflicts of the policy actors, this theory asserts, wing their way into the substantive core and, in so doing, politicize it. Nelkin (1977) and others (Mazur 1981, Dean 1981), in following this interpretation, have stressed that conflicting political values will so permeate experts' discussion as to thwart any consensus on what meaning and significance is to be attached to the facts. From this perspective, factual disputes over scientific and technical evidence do not require explicit attention; it is assumed that they can be fully accounted for in terms of the conflicting evaluations that the experts bring with them to the technical debate.

Nelkin, for instance (in her studies of the disputes surrounding the Cayuga Lake nuclear installation (1971) and the proposed new runway at Boston Airport (1974a)), concludes that the acceptance of certain technical data depends largely on 'the extent to which it reinforces existing [political] positions'. Mazur (in his analyses of scientific disputes over fluoridation and radiation) similarly singles out the political context of the controversies as the crucial determinant of the way scientific and technical data are used as political resources (Mazur 1973, 1981). Both Nelkin and Mazur, who between them have done so much to develop the whole study of technological decision making, have been content to go along with the mainstream of political science. In accepting the politics of interest paradigm, they have attributed the conflicts between technical experts squarely to their *pre-existing* political stances. However, as they have pushed this mode of analysis into more and more cases of technological decision making, they have gradually revealed its limitations.

Thanks to their work, we can now see that the established interpretation of technological decision controversies rests on a purely *instrumental* view of the politicization of technical expertise. In this view, 'factual' knowledge and 'expert' evidence, though they belong to the substantive core, are used to challenge, as well as to promote, preferred technological decisions. Their work has also shown that, often enough, such debates, rather than helping to bring about the closure of political controversies, actually intensify them. Nelkin, for instance (in her study of the Cayuga Lake siting dispute) clearly shows how the disagreement among the policy actors could not be settled by the rational debate among the scientific experts on 'technical' issues of 'fact' (Nelkin 1971). This research, in revealing that the substantive core is neither substantive nor core-like, has called into question the whole framework – the politics of interest – on which it has been founded. Since this is the framework we wish to dismantle, and to replace with something better, we will examine it more closely.

The Conventional Framework

The politics of interest approach insists that competing policy actors, representing conflicting value premises, will manipulate factual uncertainties and ambiguities for their respective ends. From this rational choice perspective, the selective use and interpretation of knowledge is not considered to be fundamentally different from what goes on in other policy debates. Depending on their pre-existing political goals, policy actors are seen as making voluntary choices about what factors to take into account and which issues to exclude. Knowledge, on this view, is *used* politically but it is not *formed* politically. Disagreement among technical experts, Mazur tells us, reflects 'simply the normal process of polarization which must be expected in any intense controversy' (Mazur 1981: 29). Similarly, Nelkin does not see technical uncertainties and scientific disagreements as analytically problematic, since controversies are typically explained in terms of the 'rational' pursuit of political goals:

> . . . in all disputes broad areas of uncertainty are open to conflicting scientific interpretation. Decisions are often made in a context of limited knowledge about potential social or environmental impacts, and there is seldom conclusive evidence to reach definitive conclusions. Thus power hinges on the ability to manipulate knowledge, to challenge the evidence presented to support particular policies, and technical expertise becomes a resource exploited by all parties to justify their political and economic views (Nelkin 1979: 16–17).

According to this conventional framework, knowledge and evidence, though often limited and inconclusive, are not themselves *rendered* limited or inconclusive by the political processes in which they are used. They may be buffeted this way and that by the conflicting values that the policy actors bring with them to the dispute, but they themselves are not generated or altered by those forces. In other words, there is no *cognitive* dimension to the political process. Although 'knowledge disputes' (Petersen and Markle 1979) have sometimes been identified as the origins of the dissensus, they have not themselves been subjected to political analysis. Fallows, for instance, in analyzing the nuclear waste controversy, has concluded that

> The disputes among experts stimulated political debate, quickly shifting the locus of decision-making from the technical to the political arena. Value questions began to override questions of technological alternatives (Fallows 1979: 105).

Ambiguities and conflicting interpretations of scientific evidence have been examined predominantly in the context of the political value disputes by which controversies have been characterized. Two basic explanations for conflicting factual evidence have been advanced. One is that scientific and technical data are themselves incomplete and inconclusive, causing experts to disagree (Gilpin 1962). The other emphasizes that disagreement among experts does not concern the scientific questions at stake, but is induced by their political views which determine how this technical evidence is interpreted (Mazur *et al.* 1979, Nowotny 1980). Either way, the ambiguous and inconclusive nature of scientific evidence is seen as the principal reason for the emergence of political conflict (Campbell 1982).

Controversy studies thus attribute an *explanatory* status to technical ambiguities and inconclusive factual data. Nelkin, for instance, contends that

> . . . technological controversies stem from factual uncertainties that allow diverse and value-laden interpretations, and technical questions become controversial largely because of the difficulty of determining the often fuzzy boundaries between facts and values (Nelkin, as quoted in Campbell 1982).

But this argument is clearly contradictory. If the boundaries between facts and values are ambiguous (or at least integral to the political debate) it is meaningless to speak of factual uncertainty as an absolute and empirical determinant for the political value conflicts that are assumed to flow from it. Indeed, by failing to integrate factual and value disputes in a single interpretative perspective, the traditional political science approach to technological decision making is both incorrect and tautological. It is incorrect in defining technical uncertainty only as the absence of complete knowledge in factual and objective terms, first because it ignores entirely the interdependence of facts and values, and, second, because it fails to account for (or even recognize the existence of) contending cognitive frames. It is tautological in promoting the idea that it is factual uncertainty that creates controversy whilst, at the same time, going along with the assertion that it is the conflicting political values of the actors that determine their factual stances in the debate.

The prevailing paradigm has got itself into this mess by its insistence that *all is conflicting interests* (Fallows 1979). Indeed, the conflict of interests in the interpretation and use of scientific and technical data has now been identified as one of the 'central findings' to have emerged from the controversy literature (Del Sesto 1983): a self-fulfilling prophecy, if ever there was one! Our argument is that, in uncritically taking their theoretical cue from the politics of interest, the students of technological decision making have excluded everything else from their field of view and then cried 'Eureka!' when that which remained visible to them conformed to their expectations. Divergent interests, hardly surprisingly, have been identified as the key determinants of conflict among policy actors. As Nelkin has typically concluded:

The outcome of many disputes depends on the relative power of competing interests. In some cases industrial interests prevail. . . . In other cases, powerful protest groups exercise sufficient leverage to determine outcome (Nelkin 1979: 19).

A major weakness in most of these studies is that the notion of competing interests is not explicitly defined. In the most general terms, interests refer to the divergent preferences of policy actors which, in turn, are typically cast in terms of the respective political values that govern their processes of assessment and choice. As Nelkin has it:

> . . . in all controversial situations, the value premises of the disputants colour their findings. The boundaries of the issues regarded as appropriate all tend to determine which data are selected as important, which facts emerge . . . Whenever judgements [about priorities or acceptable risk] conflict, this is reflected in the selective use of technical knowledge (Nelkin 1979: 16).

The traditional approach, given its emphasis on political value conflicts, is characterized by a linear, causal model of dissensus. In treating competing interests as the key explanatory variables it gives us, in Rip's words, a 'dope model' of controversies: policy actors are 'doped' by their political alignments (Rip 1984). These political predispositions, in turn, determine the way the actors identify impacts, the way they interpret and use scientific evidence, and how they select the criteria for judging the acceptability of a technology.

This dope model makes clear the basic features, and limitations, of the traditional rational choice perspective on policy-making. It argues from the independently formulated political ends of conflicting policy actors to the voluntary choice of technological means in the rational pursuit of those ends. In the next chapter we will step back from the minutiae of technological decision making and examine this dominant political model in basic theoretical terms. Since our argument is that the redefinition of technology – in particular, its loss of aloofness – has profound implications for our understanding of the nature of politics, we will conclude this chapter by summarizing the analytic limitations of this approach, as manifest in the mainstream empirical literature on technological decision controversies.

The Two-Party Adversarial Frame

The view that all is conflicting interests has led analysts to a too simple polarization of actors into opponents and proponents. Their argument is that as policy actors are doped by their pre-existing political alignments so they come down for or against any particular technology. This, as Rip (1984) has argued, is one of the regrettable blind spots in the prevailing paradigm of controversy studies. It leaves the substantive core – the technology itself – unquestioned and, in insisting that actors either support or oppose it, denies the possibility of their 'entering into' the technology (as happened with the lavatory rim-blocks) and modifying it so that it gives them rather more of what they like about it and rather less of what they dislike. In other words, the dope model is a seriously impoverished account of a rich, untidy and opportunity-filled process. It depicts well-rounded actors as cardboard cut-outs, and it totally ignores the endless, piecemeal interventions by which our technologies actually come into existence and, once in existence, develop.

In Nelkin's analysis, for instance, the different policy views and technology assessments are cast explicitly in terms of polarized statements and claims between proponents (such as developers and their technical consultants) and opponents (such as citizen groups and counter-experts) (Nelkin 1975). Mazur goes even further and frames technical controversies in terms of partisans, with 'one side favouring a technology and another opposing it'. Within this frame, the various claims and arguments that are brought to a policy debate are seen as imperative to the respective political alignments of the policy actors (Mazur 1981: 62). The trouble with this frame, empirically, is that actors who find themselves on the same 'side' often turn out to have very different political alignments (and vice versa). On the theoretical front, things are even worse because the analysis turns out to be nothing more than the restatement of the premise. For instance, Mazur concludes (with reference to the nuclear power debate) that 'proponents compared to opponents see a greater need for nuclear power, greater benefits flowing from it and smaller risk'. Opponents, for their part, 'necessarily' disagree with these assessments (Mazur 1981).

Redescription, alas, is not analysis. If we are to have analysis then we will have to go beyond the dope model and enquire into the social and cognitive premises that underpin the value positions that are taken up by the contending actors. We are not arguing that policy actors do not *have* self-evident interests; only that this is not *all* they have. Since it is by enquiring into that which is there but is not self-evident that we escape from the redescription loop, we concur with those who have argued that the analysis of technological debates should be devoted to 'unravelling the evaluational bases of competing interests' (Del Sesto 1983: 413). To accept that proclaimed policy preferences can be taken at face value without further analysis is, we insist, to remain trapped in the dope model.

Escaping from the Redescription Loop

If interests, above and beyond that part of them that is self-evident, have a social and cognitive basis then policy debates cannot be seen as being made up of separately defined social ends that then provide the evaluative premises for the rational and voluntaristic selection of technological means. Yet this is what the dominant political model (the politics of interest, for instance, the dope model and the rational choice model) insists is going on. Since we, of course, are not the first to have pointed this out, we will now pave the way for the new model we wish to establish by summarizing some of the criticisms that have already been levelled at the conventional model.

Tribe, in the context of environmental impact assessments, has stressed the empirical reality of 'means–end fluidity', and has shown how the identification of the relevant factual dimensions and the evaluative criteria evolve as an *interactive* process in the course of policy determination (Tribe 1976). Wynne, similarly, has argued that 'technological decisions, which we usually suppose to be subject to a coherent and independently formulated frame of social values, actually influence the shape of dominant social values themselves' (Wynne 1980, 1983, Winner 1977, 1980, Tribe 1973). If means and ends are to some extent merged then they cannot be entirely separate in the way the conventional model insists that they are. Similarly, if technological decisions, far from being distinct from the social values that shape them, actually enter into and change those values then the whole idea of a substantive core – the idea on which technological decision making is founded – goes out of the window. In other words (as we argued in Chapter 1) politics, technology and social choice are an inchoate entanglement and, therefore, can never be fitted into any frame that insists that they are choate.

Some analysts have now begun to address this serious analytic deficiency by taking to task the underlying assumption that controversies are about political values that are brought to bear upon *the* problem of technology. For too long, they point out, the rational perspective has ignored the potential for disagreement among policy actors about the exact *nature* of the technological issue at stake. Technology, they insist, is never just a neutral tool; it always bears the imprint of the social anvil on which it was forged. 'Technology', they insist, swinging to the opposite pole to the neutralists, '*is* social relations'. This, of course, is the social construction critique of the claimed objectivity of scientific knowledge extended to technology (Bijker *et al.* 1987) and, whilst we are happy to go much of the way (but not all the way) with it, our main concern here is not so much with it as with the policy-analytic shortcomings of the prevailing neutralist interpretation of technology that it rightly criticizes.

If different actors, in the same debate, cognize differently (that is, if they *see* things differently and *know* things differently), then they will inevitably be operating with different definitions of what is there. The debate, therefore, will entail the clash of differently drawn boundaries and the contention of incompatible rules of closure. Means and ends, substantive cores, facts and values, are weapons that the protagonists reach for (and define, each to his own satisfaction) *not* concepts in terms of which the debate itself can be analyzed. It is the competing *problem definitions*, and their institutional origins, that give us the measure of the debate.

Definitional issues, however, are not easily got at, once a controversy has surfaced. By contrast, there is little difficulty in finding out the terms of the ensuing debate, observing the formal structure of the policy agenda, recording who is in favour and who is against, and so on. Hardly surprisingly, redescription has largely triumphed over analysis, and forays into the definitional underpinnings have been undertaken only by those who have lived, year in, year out, with their chosen debate. One of these is Amory Lovins, who has now lived with the energy debate long enough to be able to see through its surface features:

> Underlying much of the energy debate is a tacit, implicit divergence on what the energy problem 'really' is. Public discourse suffers because our society has mechanisms only for resolving conflicting interests, not conflicting views of reality, so we seldom notice that these perceptions differ markedly (Lovins 1977).

If we were preachers we could take Lovins's *cri de coeur* as our text.

Our mission, we could say, is threefold. First, to reverse the attention paid to surface effects and the seldom-noticed perceptions of reality that, in fact, generate those effects. Second, to provide a theory of those contradictory perceptions; a theory capable of predicting how many of them there are, how they differ, why they differ, what it is that leads some policy actors to one and others to others, and how it is that no single one of these perceptions ever permanently triumphs over the rest. Third, to provide (or, if they already exist, to reveal) the social mechanisms for dealing with and making the most of these conflicting views of reality. The second and third parts – the cultural theory that accounts for the contradictory certainties, and the policy implications of that theory – we will come to in later chapters. Here our efforts are directed to the first part: shifting the focus away from the controversies themselves and onto the plural definitions that make them possible. We will use as our example the long-running and widespread controversy over nuclear power.

From Phenomena to the Possibility of Phenomena

Even in those cases where the presence of divergent problem definitions has been recognized empirically, the adherence to a linear, two-party framework based on political alignments has obscured the fundamental questions about what factors determine problem formulations. For instance, Nelkin and Pollak (in their study of the anti-nuclear movements in France and West Germany) clearly acknowledge differing frames among contending actors:

> Nuclear critics see the social and political consequences of nuclear power through very different lenses than the promoters of this technology. Their vision diverges on such varied issues as energy dependence, safety, and civil liberties (Nelkin and Pollak 1982: 194).

That Nelkin and Pollak succeed in distilling from the nuclear debate some of the main features that characterize conflicting perceptions can be seen from Table 3.1

Unfortunately (as is also clearly visible in the two columns of their table) these features are subjugated to the dope model: the linear, two-party framework of opponents and proponents. Instead of teasing out the various problem definitions, and then using them to explain the different positions taken up by the various policy actors, Nelkin and Pollak reverse the direction of explanation and

Table 3.1 Conflicting perceptions in the nuclear debate, as identified by Nelkin and Pollak.

Anti-nuclear analysis	Pro-nuclear analysis
Political consequences	
Government and industry are in collusion with little reference to broader political goals.	Government and industry only serve to implement agreed-upon political objectives.
Nuclear power implies dangerous concentration of political power and an omnipotent bureaucracy.	Government acts in the public interest. Bureaucracy is necessary for efficiency.
Nuclear power encourages proliferation and can lead to war.	Availability of energy reduces international tension.
Economic and social consequences	
Nuclear power reinforces dependence on American technology.	Nuclear power reinforces national independence.
Nuclear power means economic concentration and further inequities.	Nuclear power is necessary for growth and full employment.
Nuclear power implies a police state that threatens civil liberties.	It is the protest and the threat of terrorism that threaten civil liberties.
Role of government	
Government should defend small units against large concentrations.	Government should defend public interest against special interests.
Government should protect future generations against harm from today's generation of energy (nuclear waste).	Government should ensure that future generations have adequate resources by conserving fossil fuels.
Role of scientific expertise	
Science can be manipulated for alternate ends.	Science is neutral.
Science can be a source of harm as well as benefit.	Science contributes to harm as progress.
The problem is one of the acceptability of risk; this limits the value of technical evidence.	Technical evidence is the only basis on which to evaluate risk.

treat the different perceptions as merely the manifestations of conflicting interests and ideologies. They have travelled all the way to the Rubicon for a fishing party!

Helga Nowotny, however, *has* succeeded in separating definitions from interests and in putting the former ahead of the latter.

One of the characteristics of controversies is that hitherto accepted social definitions lose their validity. Shifts occur in what is considered the problem, as well as in what are defined as solutions. . . . Hence the debate takes place in the context of a number of problem definitions and frameworks for resolution, which only partly intersect; their premises are of a cognitive, social and political nature. (Nowotny 1979: 200; original in German)

Similarly, much recent work in the sociology of knowledge argues that processes of social differentiation are, at the same time, cognitive differentiations (Barnes and Edge 1982). Facts and values, therefore, can never be fully and clearly separated. The different premises that characterize competing policy actors will not just 'colour' the value disputes; they will inevitably affect the domains of the factual disputes as well. Wynne, for instance, has shown that 'even if the facts are well-established, it is the interpretive framework, defining the relevance of the facts, which may exert more influence on a policy-related judgement than the facts themselves' (Wynne 1982: 127).

Increasingly, the positivist assumption that scientific knowledge is a direct reflection of reality, quite separate from the social and cognitive dimensions on which its political use depends, is being contradicted by the empirical evidence. Robbins and Johnston (1976), for instance, in their study of the controversy over the health effects of low-level lead exposure, have shown that the disputants not only evaluated data differently, and derived contrary policy implications from the same or similar evidence, but that their cognitive frames produced different facts. Similarly, Campbell's (1982) study of the scientific disputes over the environmental risks of the proposed Mackenzie Valley pipeline (from Arctic Canada to the United States) concluded that different cognitive definitions of where the boundaries of the technological system under investigation lay were at the very centre of the dispute. One expert's narrow technical issue, he showed, was another expert's broader external concern.

As all this evidence has built up against the conventional facts–values divide it has stimulated the quest for some theoretical peg on which to hang this reality of the interpenetration of these two domains. Del Sesto, for instance, has argued that political dissensus should be attributed to 'competing social groups [that] attempt to impose their "world views" as cognitive non-evaluative definitions of reality'. He further points out that since some groups are better equipped to achieve this than others, this cognitive contest is deeply political in nature. (Del Sesto 1983: 409).

This deep mode of political analysis that Del Sesto has called for has now started to appear. Wynne, for instance, in his analysis of the Windscale public inquiry (into the proposal for reprocessing nuclear waste in Britain), begins with the divergent definitions of what the problem is.

> Here was a conflicting choice of technology or problem definition, which was not a 'facts' versus 'emotions' division. Nor was it clearly perceived and debated in the inquiry as a conflict of founding problem definitions. Yet the conflicting, equally legitimate definitions were a symmetrical pair based upon the different behavioural judgements and objective social experiences of the contending groups (Wynne 1984: 20).

The key area of dissensus, Wynne has shown, was between the narrow definition of the 'objective' risks of a single reprocessing plant (as institutionalized in the formal agenda of the inquiry) and the much broader issue of the proliferation of nuclear power (and even of nuclear weapons). Since institutional distrust ('no more territorial claims' versus the 'thin end of the wedge') was at the heart of this conflict, the inquiry, by insisting from the start that one side's facts were *the* facts, could do little to resolve it.

Similarly, Nowotny, in her account of the debate over nuclear power in Austria, has taken the same definitional approach. Rather than following Nelkin and Pollak, and collapsing the conflicting assessments of nuclear technology onto a single 'pro versus anti' dimension, she teases out the various divergent perceptions as they are manifested in different basic expectations, different levels of confidence in technical solutions, different risk criteria, and different impact assessments, as well as in different policy preferences. This enables her to avoid the redescription trap (in which proponents self-evidently cite the advantages of the technology and opponents emphasize its negative consequences) and to show that all the contending policy actors argue in terms of negative and positive attributes. They differ, however, on their definitions. (Nowotny 1979).

That the definitions are there (and that they are the generators of the controversies) is no longer in any doubt, but what is it that puts them there and keeps them there? The very success of Wynne and Nowotny[1] in transferring the focus of attention away from the self-evident interests, and onto the far from obvious definitions of what the problem *is*, has revealed a gaping hole, not just in the conceptual clothing of those who study technological decision making, but within the whole fabric of sociological and political theory on which those analysts draw.[2] It is to this serious deficiency that we now turn our attention.

Notes

1. And, we should add, of Rayner and Cantor (1987).

2. That theory *matters* (other than to the theorist, that is) is a vexed point. Those who believe that it does will insist that 'right acting requires right thinking' – a view that is contradicted every time we say of some decision maker: 'He did the right thing for all the wrong reasons'. However, if decision makers use analyses (either in arriving at their decisions or in justifying them) then the theories that underlie those analyses are certainly *involved* in the decision process.

   If decision makers become dissatisfied with the analyses they are offered, and begin to trust more in their own hands-on experience and in the mediating skills that that experience fosters, then theory will matter less and less. In a situation such as this – a situation which, we will be arguing, is now becoming more and more common – it is theory that will have to do the catching up. Even if his theory-less decisions are spot-on, they still have to be justified, and the decision maker's appeal, 'Just trust me', will not go on working indefinitely. Sooner or later, he will need a decent theory.

Chapter 4

Beyond the Politics of Interest

Most political theorists share the basic assumption that the pursuit of self-interest lies at the heart of political behaviour. In consequence, theoretical approaches in political analysis, diverse though they may be, can all be assembled under one rubric: the politics of interest. In this perspective the political realm is seen as an arena into which individual or group interests enter in some fashion, to be dealt with by certain processes and to be transformed into outcomes, policies or outputs (Cochran 1973). This notion of political processes treats political society, not as a single entity – a community – but as fragmented into groups that are distinguished by their respective interests. On this view, groups and their interests constitute the essence of politics, providing the conceptual terms in which political behaviour is to be explained.

This idea of politics as the conflict of interests has been widely reflected in the work of political theorists during the past decades. Indeed, the characterization of political behaviour in terms of competing preferences for actions, demands or wants – in short, interests – is sufficiently prevalent in modern political science for us to be able to argue that the pursuit of interest remains the dominant assumption in the analysis of political events. We will question this assumption, arguing that it is unsatisfying as a conceptual premise for understanding political action, that it sets up a circular explanation of distressingly small circumference, and that, since an alternative formulation is available, we are not forced to remain trapped within it.

The Politics of Interest

Policy analysts and decision theorists alike have largely concerned themselves with examining the 'logic' of political decision making in terms of competing interest. Analyses of the determinants for political behaviour have reflected this conceptual focus, and the dominance of the politics of interest is inherent in much of the political science literature. Various kinds of interest definitions can be found among political theorists concerned with the essence of politics. Their number and prevalence supports the claim that they share a basic common premise about the nature of political events.

Lasswell, in his classic book (1958), sees the political arena as being occupied by political actors who, having certain base values, demands and political strategies, attempt to achieve specified outcomes which are seen to maximize their 'value indulgences'. For Lasswell individuals and groups of individuals are moved by fundamental goals and objectives that they seek to achieve. Their desired value patterns provide the motivating force for action and choice. Value preferences are also considered the key to the formation of coalitions, arising out of the aggregation of interests whenever there is a substantial degree of overlap (Young 1968: 66). The interest premise in political theory is also reflected in David Easton's highly influential definition of political events as those concerned with 'the authoritative allocations of values for a society' (Easton 1965). It is fundamentally dependent on an understanding of values as preferences or demands held by those involved in political society.

The politics of interest readily includes the interest group theories of Bentley, Truman, Latham and others who have made group interests the main characteristic and *raison d'être* of organizations. In the words of Arthur Bentley, the founder of group theory in political science, 'there is no group without its interests' (Bentley 1949: 211). The notions of goals and goal attainment are likewise fundamental to the group approach to society. Group actors involved in political processes are seen as being impelled, by their respective interests and claims upon the other actors in the system, to participate in the group struggle that constitutes society. In this perspective the drive for goal attainment, or goal seeking, is accepted as the single most important motivating force of the political process. It is seen as the essence of politics.

Common to all theoretical statements involving interest politics is the idea that each political actor has a set of preferences and associated goals that determine his or her behaviour. This interest bias in political science is particularly striking in the analysis of policy making and political choice.

Public policy has been defined as a set of interrelated decisions taken by political actors concerning the selection of goals and the means of achieving them (Jenkins 1978: 15). Within the politics of interest, policy analysis is reduced to explaining actors' behaviour in relation to the interests displayed by each policy actor. Interest theories of political behaviour are purposive, with the policy goals taken as given. They assume that attention to particular aspects of issues, and the selection of policy options, follow preferences (as identified by each policy actor). Policy actors' respective interests are somehow accepted as being self-evident; they are the *premise* of most political analysis (Garson 1978).

The good lie

Political scientists are a disputatious lot, yet they have been remarkably reticent over the limitations of their various analytical models based on the politics of interest (Cochran 1971). The concept of interest itself has not been properly scrutinized for the theoretical assumptions that underpin its use in politics and decision making. There has been no real attempt, for example, to clarify the relationships between economic and non-economic interests, between egotistic and non-egotistic interests, or between individual and group interests on the one hand, and the more general social interests that transcend them on the other. But, even though political scientists may have tacitly agreed not to poke about in the foundations of the edifice they all inhabit, cracks have started to appear. The politics of interest model is more and more under stress in relation to the empirical reality of political phenomena.

Politics of interest models consider interests as psychological facts; simply as behaviour without any reference to the social contexts impinging upon the states of mind of the actors. Cochran, for example, has said of this reductionist approach:

> The politics of interest, following the lead of modern natural science, ignores the reality of purpose and thus is incapable of understanding the total experience of political life. Indeed, one of the manifestations of the politics of interest is its definition of politics without reference to purpose (Cochran 1971).

In the broader context of policy analysis, but in similar vein, Majone has criticized 'causal' theories of policy making of which the politics of interest may be seen as a prime example. He has argued that causal accounts of political behaviour seriously restrict the range of questions that can and should be asked about the policy process (Majone 1985). Majone has specifically identified the shortcomings of traditional policy analysis by pointing to the processes of legitimation and consensus building that are considered so essential for policy viability. He argues that policy analysis should move beyond the limited utilitarian perspective where success or failure in policy choice is considered to be dependent solely on whether it correctly determines the actions required to achieve a given goal.

The politics of interest fails to deal with the issue of policy viability because it considers the determinants of goal maximization in a social and cultural vacuum. The major limitation of this theoretical conceptualization is the assumption of the pre-existence of the preferences held by policy actors. The pursuit of self-interest as premise for policy choice assigns to the decision maker a position devoid of social relations: each policy maker will act singularly on the basis of the merits of alternatives in relation to his self-proclaimed objectives. Majone rightly points out that the practice of public policy making is seriously at odds with this theoretical perspective:

> In public life to decide, even to decide rationally, is not enough: decisions must always be justified. However whimsically policy actors come to their conclusions, good reasons have to be given for their preferences if they are to be taken seriously in the forums of public deliberations (Majone 1985, ch. 4).

Policy analysis within the confines of the politics of interest has overstated its singular concern with policy action as the selection of the best means to achieve a given end. In this limited perspective, rationality in decision means maximizing something; it means selecting the best alternative, subject to a pre-existing set of constraints (Majone 1982: 321)

To understand the limitations of such a goal-seeking model of social choice we will have to examine the notion of rationality that sustains it. Can rationality exist in a social and cultural vacuum? Can a model of social choice that is predicated on isolated decision makers – automata that arrive miraculously upon the political scene completely equipped with pre-programmed goals – tell us anything about political life in society? Are not 'rational' models of decision making coming to the end of their explanatory life if they prove unable to handle the inescapable social environment on which politics depends?

Decision Rationality and the Pursuit of Interest

Theoretical models of decision making and rationality have been numerous. Rather than reiterating the well established decision making literature (which would, in any case, go beyond the scope of this book) the discussion below will be cast in terms of the two headings under which much of the decision theoretical literature has conventionally been organized. The conceptual models concerned with rational decision making and those dealing with incrementalism are conventionally presented as poles on some theoretical continuum. A third group of 'mixed' theoretical approaches has been positioned in between as partial criticisms, as well as refinements of, the two polar models. This range of three clusters of theoretical models of policy making will serve as our framework for reviewing the theoretical literature on decision making and rationality, with the specific aim of exposing the extent to which the various models are dependent on some notion of the pursuit of goal attainment as the premise for policy actions.

The first pole

Rational decision-making models consider policy as effective goal achievement or goal maximization: a rational decision is one that most effectively achieves a given end. Simon has phrased the classic notion of synoptic rationality in public decision making as follows:

> The task of rational decision is to select that one of the strategies which is followed by the preferred set of consequences (Simon 1947).

More precisely, as to the steps or activities involved in making a decision in the rational–synoptic mode, March and Simon have provided the following descriptions:

> [The decision maker] has laid out before him the whole set of alternatives from which he will choose action . . . to each alternative is attached a set of consequences. . . . At the outset the decision-maker has a utility function or a preference ordering that ranks all sets of

alternatives from the most preferred to the least preferred. . . . The decision-maker selects the alternative leading to the preferred set of consequences. (March and Simon 1958).

In their most extreme form, models of synoptic rational decision making are based on comprehensive knowledge of all possible policy options and their consequences, as well as of the desired goals and values which make up the 'utility function'. It is the choice of the best means to desirable ends.

The criticism levelled at the rational synoptic model has been most pronounced in relation to public policy making, and centres around the assumptions that have to be prerequisite for the process of rational choice in policy making, namely:

(a)   carrying out a comprehensive comparison of all alternative policy options and all their consequences, and
(b)   finding agreement on a single set of collective ends or values that are to be maximized.

Lindblom has been the most prominent policy theorist among critics of the ideal of synoptic rationality, arguing that:

> Too many interacting values are at stake, too many possible alternatives, too many consequences to be traced through an uncertain future – the best we can do is partial analysis (Lindblom 1979).

These practical objections to the synoptic rational model as a description of policy-making behaviour, have not remained unanswered in the rationality literature, and the 'modifications' that have been made to the notion of rationality in decision making have further exposed the behavioural assumptions that underlie the rationalist models. Simon himself has introduced the notion of *bounded rationality*, conceding that 'it is obviously impossible for the individual to know all his alternatives and all his consequences (Simon 1947, 2nd edn 1957: 198). Bounded rationality allows for ways of limiting the number of policy options that are being compared and evaluated.

At the heart of the process of decision making is thus some form of closure; some restriction on the number of variables and options that are included in policy making. The essential issue in relation to the analysis of policy behaviour thereby shifts towards finding explanations for the imposition of boundaries on the scope of decisions under consideration. The choice of *rules of closure* will inevitably have a direct impact upon the outcome of any policy-making exercise (Gershuny 1978).

Indeed, proponents of the rational school of policy making have come to accept that they are using a model of 'limited' or 'partial' rationality that takes into account only some alternatives, and some consequences, related to some objectives (Carley 1981). Simon himself has advanced three procedures for closure:

(a) decision makers ignoring those consequences that are not of interest,
(b) 'satisficing', by choosing a satisfactory rather than a single optimal policy, and
(c) adjusting scopes of concern in the light of experience from earlier decisions (Simon 1947).

Whatever strategy is followed to limit the scope of analysis, the crux of the matter is that it is assumed that agreement can be reached on the set of goals and objectives (of an organization or a community) that are being pursued. The fact that attempts at a comprehensive comparison of alternatives is meaningless *unless* there is prior agreement on the criteria for evaluation, leads us to the second objection of the rationalist model of policy making: the need for consensus on ends.

This objection stems from Arrow's (1954) demonstration of the impossibility of a 'social welfare function' in public decision making; that is, a preference ranking by society on some set of alternative options. Lindblom, again, can be cited as representing the major political theory attack on the rationalist contention that agreement on a social welfare function is possible. In his words:

> In synoptic analysis the common requirement that values be clarified and systematised in advance of analysis is impossible to meet in many circumstances . . . disagreement on values guarantees that no stated principles or welfare function can command agreement. . . .(Lindblom 1965: 130–40).

This theoretical objection to rational decisions, on the grounds that it is impossible to find agreement within society over the set of values to be embodied in policy making, has shifted the whole emphasis of policy analysis away from a *single* welfare function for society.

It has been argued, for example, that a form of rationality can still be aimed for in the absence of a social welfare function, as long as the decisions are 'vindicated', so that consensus is reached on the *process* by which decisions are arrived at when disagreements persist on the desired outcome of policies (Gershuny 1978, 1981). In this perspective, the notion of rational decision making is modified in such a way as to remove the requirement for a social welfare function; for it is substituted the policy maker's own preferences.

Reluctant to concede outright that a social welfare function should not be aimed for, proponents of rational decision making have asserted that only a 'working social welfare function' is required to provide a set of objectives. In this view the optimization of such a function is the aim of rational decision making. When they subsequently assert, however, that 'alternative functions are the stuff of political opposition'(Cutt 1975: 226), it becomes obvious that here too prior agreement on a set of values to be pursued is no longer guaranteed, or expected.

Following such 'modifications' of the rational model of decision making to their logical conclusion has important implications for policy analysis: the set of goals being pursued becomes, in principle, open for negotiation. Competition between alternative goals is allowed to become a central feature of political decision making, and in the process the notion of rationality is reduced to its narrowest form. Simon has emphasized that the 'substantive rationality' by which policy actors make choices can only relate to the adoption of appropriate means to achieve preferred ends. In his words,'. . . the rationality of behaviour depends on the actor in only one respect – his goals' (Simon 1976).

With every policy actor in the decision-making process (in this definition) attempting to behave 'rationally' with respect to his own goals, the outcome of political decision making comes to be viewed as a struggle over which of the competing objectives are to be pursued. The central question from such a pluralist view of rationality in decision making becomes: 'whose welfare function?'. With the rationalist model of political decision making no longer dependent on the adoption of a single agreed utility function for society, the arena of public policy making is seen to be made up of different actors attempting to pursue their respective goals. Consequently, it is only one step removed from Lindblom's incrementalist conception of 'partisan mutual adjustment' in policy making. The rules of closure in the context of Simon's bounded rationality are thus made dependent on the particular set of preferences which is being adopted in decision making. The comparison of policy alternatives (in whatever form) and their evaluation will be based on the rankings of objectives of policy actors. The process of public decision making thus becomes the product of interacting policy actors pursuing different interests – in short, the politics of interest.

The second pole

The incrementalist mode of policy making, whilst rejecting the rationalist idea that decisions are based on a sequential means–ends distinction (of first isolating ends, followed by a selection of means), is similarly committed to a notion of the pursuit of self-interest by each policy actor. So incrementalist theorists are in fundamental agreement with the idea of bounded rationality in so far as they acknowledge that, in choosing which policy option to adopt, it is necessary to make reference to a limited set of alternatives namely, those that are seen to be in the actor's interest.

Lindblom introduced the idea of partisan mutual adjustment to emphasize that decisions are the product of give and take among numerous participants in the policy process (Lindblom 1959). Competing interests and policy preferences are at the heart of his model. A major idea underpinning this incrementalist model of 'successive limited comparison' of policy options is that decision making is concerned with finding agreement between groups. Lindblom's recipes for incremental policy changes, and 'muddling through', are explicitly designed to minimize the expected disagreement among policy actors, each behaving in his own self-interest (Braybrooke and Lindblom 1963). In relation to our concern for policy analysis, the degree of convergence between the underlying assumptions of the two poles of the theoretical continuum is considerable. Whilst the rationalist school stresses the possibility of reaching agreement among policy actors on ends (which can subsequently be pursued through the selection of appropriate means), the incrementalist model of decision making depends on achieving mutual consensus (through bargaining and incremental adjustments) between groups of policy actors on outcomes. Both models, however, are squarely based on political decision making as consisting of some sort of balancing of interests (or preferences) represented by policy actors.

The third cluster

The difference between the two theoretical models lies largely in their differing conceptions of the feasibility of different policy-making strategies (that is, in different notions of how options can be limited in ways that will result in manageable and acceptable decisions).[1] But this is not relevant to our concern, nor to the determinants of policy behaviour. What we are interested in is identifying the underlying behavioural assumptions about the policy actors' motivations. In this respect, both the rationalist and incrementalist models embody assumptions that policy actors will try to act in their own self-interest. Their arguments are dependent on a shared conception of goal seeking in decision making. This common ground between the motivational underpinnings of the rationalist and incrementalist models of decision making is also reflected in a third cluster of conceptualizations of policy making that seeks to combine the two. Whilst this part of the theoretical literature has a more normative rather than empirical bias, the central concern with preferences and goal seeking by policy actors remains significant. The 'mixed scanning' model (Etzioni 1968), the 'optimal rational decision-making' model (Dror 1968, 1976), as well as the elaborations of the 'iterative mixed scanning' model (Gershuny 1978) share a common focus. They are all concerned essentially with avoiding the exclusion of desirable policy options from consideration as a result of restrictive closures in decision making (such as those inherent in incrementalist adjustment), whilst acknowledging that some notion of bounded rationality (i.e., the adoption of certain rules of closure) is inevitable in policy making.

The key to these approaches is to combine rationalist and incrementalist techniques in order to select rules of closure so as to include those policy options which are in the interest of the policy makers. The interests which are pursued in decision making are at the heart of these conceptualizations. Disagreement on values (that is, conflicting interests) are thereby seen to lead to alternative choices of the rules of closure in the inevitable process of limiting the scope and nature of analyzing policy alternatives.

In summary, it must be concluded that the pursuit of interest as the key to understanding political behaviour constitutes the central underlying assumption common to the main body of theoretical models of the process of public decision making. This is also reflected in the way policy analysis has empirically focused on explaining policy outcomes in terms of the interactions between policy actors pursuing their respective interests. Central to these approaches has been the idea that actors' interests provide a self-evident starting point from which purposive behaviour can be studied scientifically. The analysis of public decision making is thereby reduced to a single level – the politics of interest – with the pre-existence of goals as its essential premise.

Beyond Interest Models of Social Choice

The theories of decision making reviewed in the previous section assume the pre-existence of preferences as providing a motivation for policy actors to select particular courses of action. They insist that the process of decision making can be understood by looking at actors' interests as prior attributes to behaviour. Individuals and organizations are expected to explain their own actions, as well as those of others, in terms of interest premises that are presumed to be antecedent to behaviour.

The fundamental deficiency of this model lies in the fact that it fails to concern itself with the origins of interest. It treats the interests adopted by policy actors as self-evident, ignoring the question as to how the alignment of particular interests and actors is actually determined. Politics of interest models of decision making cannot handle the question: 'how do policy actors who behave in their own best interest come to know where that interest lies?'.

Policy actors trying to determine what their interests are can only do so with reference to certain rules of closure, but the setting of these boundaries on analysis and choice has itself been considered (within the politics of interest model) an action requiring reference to a policy actor's goals. In other words, any attempt at determining one's own best interest is itself dependent on prior knowledge of the set of objectives which are being pursued. In short, to know one's own interest one must know one's own interest.[2] It is at this point that any model premised on predetermined interests breaks down as an analytical basis for explaining political events and the particular positions that policy actors take up in decision making.

The cause of this total breakdown (for that is what it is) is political science's neglect of purpose. It has failed at four crucial points. First, it has focused on goal seeking and disregarded goal setting. Second, it has ignored the need for decisions to be morally justifiable. Third, it has treated rationality as extensional, as having an existence that is independent of organizational context. Fourth, it has viewed social institutions as aggregations of individuals and not as cultural entities.

Goal seeking and goal setting

Interest–premise theories of decision making are too tidy and ignore the dynamics and ambiguity involved in policy processes. Goals can change over time. Hence conceptual models for the analysis of decision making will have to move beyond theories of goal seeking in order to be able to account for the processes of goal setting. To move beyond the limitations of the politics of interest model, it is necessary to place the process of goal maximization in a broader context that looks for determinants of policy objectives outside the utilitarian means–ends scheme of traditional decision theories. In other words, if we want to avoid the pitfalls of such a circular goal-seeking notion of rational decision making, we will have to acknowledge the social and cultural context as the determining factor in setting boundaries to the rules of closure which are adopted by policy actors.

Of course, one way of trying to overcome the problem of predetermined goals in models of political decision making (which presuppose that outcomes reflect purely the pursuit of interest) is to take a totally relativistic approach. On can simply move away from the assumption that decision outcomes are necessarily intentional. In this view, policy actions are no longer dominated by the intentions of goal-seeking actors. Such an approach leads to a conceptualization of decision making in a context of anarchy, based on a fluidity and an ambiguity of goals. March and Olsen have formulated such a 'garbage can model' of decision making, built on the belief that the 'processes and outcomes are likely to appear to have no close relation with the explicit intention of actors' (March and Olsen 1976: 37).

Such a model views the process of decision making as a mixture of problems, solutions, policy actors and choice opportunities. It provides a conceptualization of how organizations operate in processes of decision making, but cannot be convincingly translated to an inter-organizational context of public decision making. It requires a view of society where coalitions between policy actors are constantly in arbitrary flux. Indeed, the whole question of which interest is linked to which particular group of policy actors becomes not only irrelevant (in the sense that objectives are fluid and ambiguous anyway and actions unintentional), but also excluded from the frame of reference. The definition of a policy actor would itself become ambiguous once the arena of decision making was seen to be made up of a complicated intermeshing of ever-changing organizational policy choices, problems and solutions.

In the 'garbage can' concept all configurations are in principle possible. It is based on a high degree of unconstrained relativism of policy actors and the way they view and evaluate policy problems. The infinite number of possible juxtapositions of policy actors with their respective goals and policy perceptions (be they fluid and ambiguous) would make any attempt at analyzing public policy choices in terms of goal dissensus among policy actors impracticable, if not meaningless. The question of enquiring into the origins of interest would be empirically unmanageable, but, above all, theoretically irrelevant.

Justification and cultural accountancy

What such an approach in terms of complete anarchy ignores, however, is that in observing actual cases of public decision making it is obvious that there is a certain degree of social stability in the system. A limited number of policy actors can be seen to be operating for significant periods of time; social organizations involved in decision making do seem to align themselves with particular policy objectives; policy choices once arrived at, become encrusted with moral justifications. It is this viability criterion of justifiability that gives rise to a certain measure of repetition in the observed phenomena. If there were no recurrent regularities in those phenomena then there would be nothing to talk about, yet the paradox is that the relativists have insisted on talking about it all without acknowledging the existence of these moral claims that are precisely what makes it possible for them to talk about it at all. In other words, a position of complete relativism fails to acknowledge that the policy actors are social organizations whose maintenance and viability depends on their accounting for their actions.

Much of the literature on decision making and rationality is based on this individualist fallacy. It has implicitly developed in the mistaken belief that its inquiry, as applied to individuals, can simply be extended to the level of social organizations. Individual choice processes, as the basic unit of analysis, may draw us initially to the belief that the pattern of rules of closure in decision making is unlimited in variation. Given that different individuals may have markedly different definitions of the situation they encounter, there could be as many goal-setting directions in their behaviour as there are individuals in the polity. At the level of policy actors as social organizations, however, rules of closure in decision making have to be made credible, and shareable, by mustering social support for the way they 'home in' on particular objectives.

The idea that some policy problems and some policy solutions can form relatively stable alliances with some policy actors in the arena of decision making, and that these are the ones that 'survive', leads us to abandon the idea of complete relativism. We can reject the garbage can model of random streams of policy actors, problems, solutions and choice opportunities, and return to the question of the origins of interests in terms of a purposive conceptual model. Acknowledging that the dynamic nature of processes of decision making indicates that a static, deterministic framework of policy behaviour is inappropriate (but that, at the same time, policy actors are subject to the stringent viability criteria of accountability, credibility and shareability), we arrive at a position of *constrained relativism*.

We are now in a position to formulate what may be called an accountancy model of interests, based on the notion that only a limited number of groups of policy actors with their particular interests can convincingly account for their actions in such a way as to be socially viable. From this perspective, we can now address the question of the origins of interest, and take aboard the significant issues of credibility and policy justification as an essential element of political decision making and social choice. In effect, we are returning here to the question of the boundaries of analysis and rules of closure in social decision making. In terms of the language of decision-making theory, we are reintroducing the question of what kinds of boundaries can occur in relation to the rationalities of policy actors operating in a social environment.

Rationality and its contexts

Although social constraints on choice situations have received only limited attention in the literature, the idea of bounded rationality does allow scope for social factors to be systematically included in the decision-making analysis. It is clear that the social environment imposes constraints upon choice and sets boundaries on the range of feasible alternatives (Douglas and Wildavsky 1982), and Simon himself has suggested that these constraints and boundaries are in some way built into the perspectives of rational decision makers:

The givens in the situation of choice (that is, the environment) and the behaviour variables (that is, the organism itself) are usually kept strictly apart, but we should be prepared to accept the possibility that what we call 'the environment' may lie, in part, within the skin of the biological organism (Simon 1955).

Once we concede that the 'organism' may to some extent create its own 'environment', we are led directly to a framework of cultural pluralism within which the self-interest of each policy actor is embedded in the environment he creates for himself. This notion of social institutions as different cultural entities, which provide both the social constraints and incentives for policy choices, is the key to a goal-setting model of decision making. The essential feature is that cultural differentiation among organizational policy actors will result in alternative socially constructed boundaries to the rules of closure governing the framing of policy problems and the selection of goals.[3] Each organizational culture will justify its policy choices in relation to the internal and external social constraints under which it operates. The boundaries to rationality thus depend on the cultural orientation of each policy actor.

Social institutions as cultural entities

At the centre of such a cultural approach to the politics of interest is the insistence that the social viability of organizations be seen primarily in terms of the construction and maintenance of shared meanings and justificatory mechanisms whereby their members collectively sustain their distinctive patterns of relationships. Organizations can thus be treated as cultures that are only viable in the social environment if they are able to ensure the commitment of their members to a particular way of making sense of the situations they encounter. Organizational cultures are viable only if people are willing and able to support them; the sustained survival of policy actors will depend on the credibility that individuals grant to them (Thompson 1982a). This idea of cultural pluralism among organizational policy actors is able to account for the process of goal selection by making reference to those incentives offered, and actions taken, which help to ensure the stability of organizational boundaries.

However, the internal world of the organization cannot be isolated from the world external to it. The moral commitment that organizational members make to a particular institutional (i.e., cultural) perspective is inextricably linked to the social context in which they operate. Any cultural orientation of an organization will be closely tied to the social context that renders it meaningful. The social environment can be viewed as the breeding ground for a particular cultural orientation, whilst at the same time the resultant socially constructed perspective provides the basis for the justification and legitimation of its position in the social world. This notion of *essential cultural pluralism* implies that each distinctive organizational culture, whilst denying alternative, institutionally induced perceptions of social reality, is in fact dependent on those divergent cultural contexts for its own survival and social viability.[4]

We have, we concede, come a long way from the utilitarian, instrumentalist, individualist assumptions about social choice that provide the largely unquestioned foundations upon which the theories of policy making and decision rationality we have surveyed here have been built. Our immodest aim is to raze that tatty structure to the ground and to build a decent one on some real foundations. What is more, we now have the specifications for those foundations: a focus on goal setting, a framework for moral justifications, a notion of rationality that is embedded in social and cultural contexts, and an idea of the individual as a social being whose individuality comes not just from within himself but also from his involvement with others. Given these specifications, it is likely that the theoretical structure we are about to erect will look quite different from the one we have just demolished.

Notes

1. The rationalists and the incrementalists, it has been argued, are not arguing about the same things. Their respective concerns, Smith and May (1980) point out, are with what ought to be attempted in decision making and what is feasible in real-life instances of policy making.

2. It is because they operate under what Dahl and Lindblom (1965: 63) have called the 'paradox of specialization' that organizations, in order to address issues, must disaggregate them, thereby ignoring some variables and focusing on a limited set of others. It is precisely because of this circularity that some normative models of public decision making, such as that advanced by Gershuny (1978), have insisted on the need for a never-ending iterative component in attempts at rational decision making.

3. A number of analysts (such as Edelman 1971, 1988) have acknowledged the social construction of political problems and the ambiguity of

definitional frames in public policy making. What they lack, as compared to our approach, is a theory of (cultural) differentiation that can account for the various forms of social construction.

4. The strength of this notion of cultural pluralism is that it is essentially a way of coming to terms with the dilemma of the relationship between cultural values and behaviour. It provides a conceptual basis for avoiding the apparent contradiction between those social theorists who consider cultural categories as reflections or by-products of social action and those who see culture as the rule book that specifies what action is possible and what is seen as credible (Thompson 1979).

Chapter 5

Political Cultures: A New Framework for Policy Analysis

W e hear much of 'the irrational and emotional fears of the public'; the opponents of nuclear power, for instance, are often dismissed in this way.[1] Yet, paradoxically, some of those opponents are seen as highly rational – the mineworkers, for instance, whose interests (jobs, security, prospects) would be much strengthened if nuclear power were phased out. So is it interests or is it irrationality? Many would say that we cannot understand policy debates until we can answer this question. We would say that we cannot understand policy debates until we stop asking this question. So we begin by asking a quite different question: what is a resource?

We were once fortunate enough to be spectators at an exchange of views on this question between two extremely distinguished scientists. One of them let drop something about 'natural resources' and the other was down on him like a ton of bricks. 'You cannot talk about natural resources' he cried, 'there are only raw materials' and he went on to explain how a raw material only becomes a resource when human ingenuity, skill and enterprise are successfully focused upon it.

This is a profound, perennial and irresolvable disagreement. For one scientist riches are given to us by nature; for the other they are given to us by our social inheritance – by that complex whole that gets transferred from one generation to the next by mechanisms that are not genetic: a whole that includes the whole of language, the whole of knowledge, the whole of technology and a great deal more besides. Clearly the two scientists locate resources very differently. Their premises, in other words, are different and, as a result, so are the sorts of policies they see as desirable (or even feasible). One has an idea of nature as something stern and unforgiving, as supplying us with a strictly accountable inventory of resources. The other sees these limitations as being of little consequence because they are capable of modification, exploitation and multiplication through the application of skills that are socially acquired and transmitted. In this way he is led to the idea of nature as essentially cornucopian.[2]

So here is a fundamental cleavage. One scientist's world is a world of resource depletion; the other's, a world of resource abundance. Since each insists that the world is constituted in a way that the other insists it cannot be, each acts in that world in a markedly different way. But, though their actions (and their policy preferences) are so dramatically different, each is perfectly rational in terms of his convictions about nature and about human nature.

This disagreement over what resources are and where they come from makes three things clear: first, that divergent behaviours can be rational; second, that we can never be completely agreed on how the world is; and third, that interests are not necessary conditions for rational behaviour. These philosophical points have immediate practical implications.

They tell us, for instance, that those who are convinced that the wastes we already have are already pointing the finger of death at thousands of children not yet born will have a quite different assessment of nuclear technology from those who would, as the saying goes, happily sprinkle that same waste on their cornflakes. The establishment's time-honoured response is that those who challenge science (by which they mean their science) and its findings are irrational; this is not just tactless (and infuriating to those it patronizes); it misses the whole point. What we have is not the real risks versus a whole lot of misperceptions of those risks but the clash of plural rationalities, each using impeccable logic to derive different conclusions (solution definitions) from different premises (problem definitions). Nor is it the calm authority of science versus the irrational and emotional fears of the public. The scientists too are divided (witness the argument over the shape of the dose–response curve at low exposures. The British Department of the Environment's scientists feel obliged to assume a linear relationship, the American organization, Scientists and Engineers for Secure Energy, latches onto the quadratic curve, whereas Alice Stewart and the Friends of the Earth favour a parabolic curve; all three are possible, given the uncertainty of the data). The outcome is a cloud of uncertainty around the scientific facts and a set of contradictory certainties about the points at issue. To explain what we mean by 'contradictory certainties' let us look a little more closely at the three dose–response curves.

These three curves cannot be reconciled. A straight line can never curve, and a curve that bends one way can never be fitted to one that bends the other way. The parabolic curve tells us that the more nuclear technology we have the more harm will befall us; the quadratic curve tells us that there will be less and less to worry about; the straight line tells us that the technology is 'neutral': that the risks it brings with it are not inevitably one way or the other – they can (and must) be managed, planned and regulated.

It is by this sort of analysis – first pinning down the irreconcilables, then looking at their stability properties to see whether things get worse, better or neither – that we can identify the contradictory certainties and relate them back to the myths of nature, of which they are particular historical manifestations. The increasing risks of the parabolic curve assign it to nature ephemeral, the decreasing risks of the quadratic curve assign it to nature benign, and the neutral and controllable risks of the straight line assign it to nature perverse/tolerant (see Figure 1.1). The holders of these three curves can similarly be assigned by institutional type: the Friends of the Earth to *egalitarian collectives* (undifferentiated bounded groups), Scientists and Engineers for Secure Energy to *markets* (ego-focused networks), and the Department of the Environment's scientists to *hierarchies* (nested bounded groups). The cultural theory tells us that it is this vital link between organization and cognition that structures and uncertainty and, in so doing, places the entire debate beyond the reach of the politics of interest.

But, for all their lack of paramountcy, interests *do* make a difference. Indeed, we scarcely need all this 'assumptional analysis' to understand those bizarre coalitions of vicars, Tory matrons and bearded vegetarians heroically manning the barricades against the developers and their fiercely enthusiastic workforces. The divergent interests of those directly affected — community disruption, falling property prices, habitat destruction, profits and jobs — go most of the way to explaining Nimbies and Lulus. What interests cannot explain, however, are the diverse passions of those, like our two distinguished scientists, who have no direct personal stake in the issue. Nimbies and Lulus may appear to cope with West German Greens protesting about West German sites for the disposal of radioactive waste, but they are no match for the next step in which the protesters seek to prevent the disposal of that same waste in the middle of the Gobi

Desert. It is this step that we are trying to get to grips with in this book.

If interest explanations are not always adequate then we will need the answers to two questions: one theoretical, the other practical.

1. How do we go beyond interests?
2. When do we need to go beyond interests?

This chapter is concerned only with answering the first question. The second question we address in Chapter 9.

The Structuring of Uncertainty

Since it is always a pretty fuzzy line that separates those who don't want the development in their own backyard from those who don't want it in anyone's backyard, and since some individuals often drift across that line in the consciousness-raising course of their involvement (whilst others stick resolutely to their local cause), interest explanations (and, in particular, the characterization of certain groups as Nimbies and certain proposals as Lulus) are often seriously wide of the mark. They encourage solutions to what are not, in fact, the problems. That is, they stimulate a search for ingenious ways of making a particular installation more palatable (by compensation payments, for instance, or cheaper electricity) and direct attention away from the need to shift the technology in question out of the unsustainable path in which it has become entrenched. Plural rationalities allow us to circumvent this pitfall. They show us that, above and beyond the various interests of the various actors, there are different convictions as to how the world is and as to how people are: different definitions of the problem and different definitions of the solution.

The trouble (as we showed in Chapter 2) is that interest-based explanations cannot cope with the dynamic shifts in credibility that accompany this fuzzy line: with local objectors, for instance, losing their faith in the centralized institutions of the state or, conversely, with long-standing critics of those institutions suddenly moving across and joining them (the co-option of troublesome outsiders, which is so marked a feature of confident and flexible establishments). These dynamics tell us that people's interests sometimes change in ways that are not at all self-evident (they also tell us that consciousness raising, contrary to much popular belief, is not always in the same single direction). What has happened in these sorts of cases is that a person has switched from one set of contradictory certainties to another: from one myth of nature to another, from one rationality to another. The big question then is: what caused the shift?

The local objector, faced with the imminent arrival of a national radioactive dump on his doorstep, finds himself flung into a kind of intense communal and egalitarian activity that previously was not a feature of his social involvement. Squire and tenant, vicar and parishioner, school teacher and pupil, indigene and newcomer, all join hands to form the human barricade; all of them, while off duty, stay close to their telephones, passing on information about approaching Nirex convoys and suspicious outsiders to all who need to know, sometimes with complete disregard for the status distinctions and personal networks that channel the flow of local information in less troubled times. In terms of cultural theory we can see that, by responding to the external threat, many of them experience a dramatic shift in social context: from wherever they were before towards the bottom right corner of our social context diagram (positive group, negative grid; see Figure 1.2). Nor, if they are successful in fighting off the threat, do they automatically fall back to where they were before. Institutional trust, once destroyed, is never that easily restored.

The troublesome critic who finds himself co-opted by the establishment has travelled in the opposite direction, abandoning the egalitarian and collective fervour of his uncompromisingly activist group for the status and influence of a specially created niche in the administrative or corporate hierarchy. The very success of his organization has enabled him, as its spokesperson or messenger, to argue its case in the august forums that are dominated by those his organization has been criticizing. The more time he spends hobnobbing with the hierarchists in the corridors of power the less time he has to sit around with those on whose behalf he speaks. It is a difficult balancing act and, somewhere along the way between equality and hierarchy, he finds that he has crossed the hidden line and now has more in common with those who are prepared to make a prestigious place for him than with those who are beginning to ask themselves why they see so little of him these days. Nor, if he eventually falls out with the hierarchy, will those that he has abandoned be prepared to forget all this and welcome him back to

	Hierarchical	Egalitarian	Individualistic	Fatalistic
Preferred way of organizing	Nested bounded group	Egalitarian bounded group	Ego-focused network	Margin
Certainty (myth of nature)	Nature perverse/ tolerant	Nature ephemeral	Nature benign	Nature capricious
Rationality	Procedural	Critical	Substantive	Fatalistic

Figure 5.1 The basic determinants of the four political cultures.

their midst. Institutional trust is like magnetism: the path by which it is built up is never the same as that by which it is broken down.

All this tells us, in a fairly informal way, that the plural rationalities are never *merely* cognitive. It tells us that the contradictory certainties are closely tied to the different ways of organizing: that each depends (literally 'hangs upon') the other. So we can say that an act is rational if it supports a person's way of organizing. And we can also say that the appropriate certainty for that person will be the one that best justifies that act. Since the rationalities and ways of organizing depend on one another, we now need a word for the complete packages they produce. Since these packages are cognitive, they are *cultural* and, since they are also busy organizing one way and disorganizing other ways, they are also *political*. They are, therefore, *political cultures* (Figure 5.1)

The central message of this diagram is that all is bias. Our knowing is biased, our acting is biased, our justifying of our actions is biased, and our judging of the actions of others is biased. Bias is to organizing as gravity is to walking about: we would be in a bad way without it. So bad, in fact, that we would have no society and no culture: no social relations and no cognition.[3]

Each of the four political cultures is a consistent package of biases. Our ideals of fairness, our views of resources, our awareness of needs, our engineering aesthetics, our ways of learning, our perceptions of risk, our definitions of pollution, our strategies for reconciling our needs and resources, and many, many more of the factors that make for conflicting assessments of what is possible and of what is desirable vary dramatically across the political cultures (we will tabulate these predictions in a moment). It is these patterns of bias, endlessly affirmed, endlessly acted upon, and endlessly pitted one against the others, that actually make policy and technology possible.

Political Cultures and Policy Analysis

Before we embarked on our cultural theory we did warn that it would look nothing like the existing analytic framework we wish to sweep away. It is, we readily admit, strong and unfamiliar meat and, for this reason, we should now pause to examine its strangeness and, perhaps, make it a little more palatable.

The case for a cultural perspective on public decision analysis arises out of the failure of the politics of interest model to come to terms with the social and cognitive dimensions of policy controversy. In order to understand adequately political conflicts over the selection and justification of policy choices, especially those concerned with controversial technologies, we will have to account for the various boundaries to rationality in social decision situations. This we can do by embracing the notion of *cultural pluralism* among institutional actors. The conceptual advance of cultural theory lies, therefore, not in the rejection of the idea of competing interests, but in making it contingent upon the culturally induced biases in perception of policy actors who are operating within a social arena that they themselves collectively shape and maintain.

The central idea is that policy actors may be classified by reference to a limited number of socially viable cultural orientations in perception and strategic choice: the four political cultures. This analytical perspective moves away from a static, unitary approach which assumes that there is agreement on the givens of the situation, whilst avoiding the totally relativistic position that gives equal plausibility to every imaginable configuration of policy actors and problem definitions. Our policy-analytic approach is premised on the idea of a small number of competing and culturally-dependent *selection biases*. Each distinct cultural orientation is seen to involve an appropriate way of selecting and vindicating how a policy issue is defined, what options and consequences are taken into account, and which evaluative criteria are to be seen as credible. We can explain these selection biases by elaborating the basic packages (ways of organizing, certainties, and rationalities) set out in Figure 5.1.

The conflicting ideas of nature (strictly accountable versus cornucopian) held by our two distinguished scientists readily map onto nature ephemeral and nature benign, respectively. But what about nature perverse/tolerant? Where nature benign encourages bold experimentation in the face of uncertainty and nature ephemeral encourages timorous forbearance, nature perverse/tolerant encourages the pursuit of certainty and predictability. If, as this myth insists, there is a boundary line between equilibrium and disequilibrium (between decreasing risk and increasing risk) then you can act boldly up to, but not beyond, that limit. Individualistic exuberance is all very well, so long as it does not go beyond that line, and this means that strong social sanctions (e.g., planning controls, statutory regulations, government intervention, caste-specific occupations to compartmentalize the labour market) will be needed to prevent this from happening. And, to apply all these necessary controls effectively, you need to know exactly where the line is. Where nature ephemeral stipulates a world of resource depletion, and nature benign a world of resource abundance, nature perverse/tolerant stipulates a world of *resource scarcity*: a positive sum game contained within precise and knowable limits.

So nature perverse/tolerant promotes a particular kind of knowledge, one that is virtually complete and divided into non-negotiable compartments. Knowledge is organized by its division into separate and autonomous disciplines (rather like the pillars of a classical temple) that are ultimately tied together by a shared (but rather general) faith in the completeness and unity of knowledge: the pediment and its harmonious marbles.[4] The other political cultures, however, promote quite different kinds of knowledge.

The egalitarian political culture cannot abide all the separation and smugness that accompanies the hierarchists' temple of knowledge. For egalitarians knowledge has to be accessible to all; it has to be all-of-a-piece ('holistic' is the word they tend to use) and, at the same time, imperfect (so that everyone can add to it and so that no one can claim to know with certainty that no harm will come of any innovation). Individualists, being pragmatic materialists – bottom-liners – are not much interested in whether knowledge is complete or incomplete, divided up or knitted together. They are interested in results; in knowledge that works. If it is explicit (like the hierarchists' science) and works, that is all right, but if it is implicit (like the green-fingered skill of the grower of prize vegetables, or the esoteric techniques of the management consultant with a good track record) they do not mind. Knowledge, for the individualist, has only to be sufficient and timely.[5]

The policy actors' myths of nature, views of resources, and kinds of knowledge then come together to define their distinctive learning styles. Individualists believe in trial and error, and their benign myth of global equilibrium assures them that, though they may lose, there is little chance of a catastrophic outcome in which everyone will lose. The egalitarians' myth tells them the exact opposite. Nature ephemeral is so precarious that free-for-all experimentation will almost certainly result in its total collapse. Trials, therefore, can go ahead only if it is certain there will be no error. Hierarchists are not keen on interrogating the unknown. For one thing, their complete knowledge denies its existence. Nor are they happy to hold back for fear of what might happen. Committed to control, they push their knowledge out ahead of their actions. They prefer, wherever possible, to look before they leap. Anticipation is their preferred way of learning.

And so, by this sort of socio-logic, we can go on and on teasing out the differences between the political cultures. Indeed, since these differences have now been teased out in all sorts of applications and analyses, there is no real need to go on doing it here. The current state of the political cultures framework can be set out in the form of a four-column chart (Table 5.1) which is simply the continuation of the basic chart already provided in Figure 5.1.

Some of the rows of this chart we have just explained, others we touched upon in Chapter 1; still others will become more apparent when we get into our chapters on the applications and implications of our theory. The main thing, at this stage in our argument, is not to understand the minutiae of every row but to see this chart as an interpretive framework that can be 'slid under' any policy debate or technological controversy that seems to be characterized by contradictory certainties as well as by the self-evident interests of those involved. It is not a substitute for detailed research; it is a way of making sense of that research when all other ways have failed.

The application of the concept of culture to political science is not new (Pye 1973, Almond and Verba 1965). The distinction of our cultural bias frame is that it is committed to a plurality of political cultures within the policy arena. Cultural theory is not in disagreement with those political theorists (Edelman 1964, 1971) who have focused on the culturally generated premises and prescriptions in political behaviour. In discussing the role of symbols as a characteristic element of a 'political culture', Elder and Cobb, for example, have explicitly acknowledged the link with cognitive processes in boundary setting:

> In defining the range of symbols that are available to give social definition to a situation, a political culture acts to limit the range of problems and problem solving alternatives that are likely to be considered, or for that matter, even entertained or recognized. . . . Culture colours perceptions and constrains problem definition. . . (Elder and Cobb 1983: 85).

However, much of political science still embraces the idea that it makes sense to talk in the singular about *the* national (or *the* local) political culture. But, increasingly, the reality of political conflicts shows us how different policy actors can have competing perceptions of the situation, and indicates that this simple singular assumption cannot be upheld. The debate over *whose* socio-cognitive problem definition should prevail is often a basic issue in political conflict; one that is likely to be critical in determining the outcome of policy controversies. Hence, our central concern with political cultures in the plural.

Moreover, in insisting on a plurality of institutional cultures, we avoid the notion of culture as a residual category in analysis: an uncaused cause that is turned to only when theory-based explanations have failed. This is not our idea of culture. Our idea allows us to develop an explanatory theory based on the variation of cultural settings *within* societies or organizations. Our idea is that social institutions construct their organizational cultures in the *process* of behaviour, that is, of decision making. Hence a plurality of political cultures provides a conceptual basis for understanding differences in behaviour within the same mode of analysis as the symbols and perceptions that accompany and justify that behaviour.

Some might try to see cultural theory as a way of enhancing the traditional approach to policy analysis by incorporating into it the view, advanced by symbolic organization theorists, that the symbols and social perceptions of reality can become a basis on which decisions are made and actions taken (Pfeffer 1981: 34). However, we would not be satisfied with this sort of 'monster adjusting' (Lakatos 1976) because it leaves too much unchanged. We advance a much stronger programme and say that decisions cannot be made and actions cannot be taken *without* such socio-cognitive supports.

Table 5.1 The four political cultures

	Hierarchical	Egalitarian	Individualistic	Fatalistic
Preferred way of organizing	Nested bounded group	Egalitarian bounded group	Ego-focused network	Margins of organized patterns
Certainty (myth of nature)	Nature perverse/tolerant	Nature ephemeral	Nature benign	Nature capricious
Rationality	Procedural	Critical	Substantive	Fatalistic
View of resources	Scarce	Depleting	Abundant	Lottery
Scope of knowledge	Almost complete and organized	Imperfect but holistic	Sufficient and timely	Irrelevant
Learning style	Anticipation	Trial without error	Trial and error	Luck
Social context	Positive group/positive grid	Positive group/negative grid	Negative group/negative grid	Negative group/positive grid
Desired systems properties	Controllability (through inherent orderliness)	Sustainability (through inherent fragility)	Exploitability (through inherent fluidity)	Copability (through inherent chaos)
Ideal scale	Large	Small	Appropriate	—
Engineering aesthetic	High-tech virtuosity	Frugal and environmentally benign	Appropriate (as cheap and cheerful as possible)	—
Ideal of fairness	Equality before the law	Equality of result	Equality of opportunity	Not on this earth
Cultural bias	Ritualism and sacrifice	Fundamentalism/millenarianism	Pragmatic materialism	Inconsistent eclecticism

	Bureaucratization through increasing transaction costs (O. Williamson)	'Buddhist' and 'thermodynamic' economics (E.F. Schumacher and N. Georgescu-Roegen)	Neo-Austrian: competition without equilibrium (F. Hayek, A. Alchian)	Marginalization through structural imbalance (neo-Marxist)
Preferred economic theory				
Energy future	Middle of the road (technical fix)	Low growth (radical change now)	Business as usual	What you don't know ...
Perception of time	Balanced distinction between short and long term	Long term dominates short term	Short term dominates long term	Involuntary myopia
Preferred form of governance	Leviathan	Jeffersonian	*Laissez-faire*	It doesn't matter who you vote for ...
Salient risks	Loss of control (i.e., of public trust)	Catastrophic, irreversible and inequitable developments	Threats to the functioning of the market	—
Model of consent	Hypothetical consent	Direct consent	Implicit consent	Non consent
Method for applying model of consent	Natural (or other ideal) standards	Expressed preferences	Revealed preferences	—
Risk-handling style	Rejection and absorption	Rejection and deflection	Acceptance and deflection	Acceptance and absorption
Latent strategy	Secure internal structure of authority	Survival of the collectivity	Preservation of the individual's freedom to contract	Survival of individual
Commitment to institutions	Correct procedures and discriminated statuses are supported for own sake. *Loyalty*	Collective moral fervour and affirmation of shared opposition to outside world. *Voice*	Only if profitable to the individual. If not, then *exit*.	—

Our notion of contending political cultures makes it explicit, and central, that social actors may be expected to differ on the kinds of symbols and issues that are seen as politically salient and on what meanings are to be attached to them. The cultural bias model then provides us with a systematic and coherent basis for recognizing, classifying and analyzing these fundamental differences that actually render policy making possible.

The Classification of Social Contexts

Our four political cultures are closely related to Mary Douglas's grid/group typology of social contexts (Douglas 1970, 1978, 1982). Traditionally (in terms of the hierarchists' temple of knowledge, that is) the individual belongs to psychology and the aggregations of individuals – families, clans, lineages, age grades, and so on – to anthropology. Douglas's great entrepreneurial achievement has been to disregard this separation and to treat the individual, not as 'an isolated psycho-physiological entity', but as a social being: someone whose individuality actually comes from his involvement with others (the traditional view, she insists, just perpetuates the 'individualist fallacy'). Her grid/group typology, therefore, is a way of classifying an individual (*not* a group of individuals, or an institution, or a society) in terms of the way in which he is involved with others. These distinct ways of involvement, she argues, achieve both their stability and separateness from the interpenetrations of social and symbolic orders that they, and only they, make possible. Each type of social involvement generates, and is sustained by, a distinct perceptual orientation. Involvement and orientation *depend upon* one another. Bias, therefore, is the inevitable and inescapable accompaniment of order.

By arguing that only a limited number of combinations of institutionally induced perceptions and social contexts are viable (that is, morally justifiable), cultural theory gives us a fourfold classification of cultural biases.[6] If we cannot escape the biases we can at least map them, and Douglas proposes the two dimensions of sociality as the means of doing this mapping (Douglas 1982, Ostrander 1982). Group and grid, as she calls them, serve to classify the two fundamental dimensions of action limited by social order: who one interacts with, and how one interacts with them. We have already set out this grid/group classification (in Chapter 1) and have shown how it connects directly with the ecologist's myths of nature, in one direction and, in the other, with the notions of contradictory certainties and plural rationalities – political cultures – that we are using to analyze policy debates, especially those over technology.

Our idea of policy analysis is that the different social and cultural environments in which policy actors operate will lead them to respond differently to decision-making situations. Our framework for that analysis, therefore, is a comparative classification of individuals' social environments as generators of different 'patterns of culture' (Benedict 1935, Geertz 1973, Smircich 1983). This framework then allows us to recognize and map the cognitive biases underlying the complex institutional behaviours that together make up the decision process. Culture in this view, is neither completely rigid, nor is it totally fluid. It is plastic. Though it can be pushed this way and it can be pushed that way, it cannot be pushed just anywhere. Cultural categories, though they are in many ways socially negotiable, also exhibit a certain stability in that only some are persistent through social experience (Thompson 1979: 216). It is these persistent strands that the four political cultures – the four columns of Table 5.1 – capture.

At the dynamic heart of these persistent strands are the two control dimensions: grid and group. Grid and group 'control' the basic choices facing individuals as social beings: who to interact with, and how to interact with them. The grid dimension is concerned with the degree of prescriptive hierarchy to which interacting individuals are subjected. It relates to the extent of interpersonal role differentiation and structural stratification impinging upon social actors.

This dimension can be visualized as running from 'egalitarian' to 'hierarchical' (or, as we show in Figure 1.2, from 'prescribing' to 'prescribed') social environments. The group dimension refers to those social contraints that relate to the degree of social incorporation (Douglas 1978: 7). It classifies the social environment according to the extent to which individual behaviour is subject to or free from the social pressures of bounded social groups. This dimension can be seen as running from 'individualized' to 'collectivized' social environments. These crossed axes[7] depict the limits against which social behaviour can be mapped, and they give us our four social beings (the individualist, the fatalist, the hierarchist and the egalitarian) whose distinct identities are obtained from the social contexts to which they belong, and which they strive to maintain.

If they cease to maintain their contexts they cease to belong, and vice versa. It is the two together – organism shaped to environment and environment shaped to organism – the theory holds, that confers viability. This is the explicit criterion for social being to be possible. This criterion, as it weeds out the non-viable conjunctions, shapes the social arena into just four distinct tendencies of social orientation: one in each of the four quadrants of the social context map. In other words, these four 'ideal types' are exhaustive; they are all the types there are.[8]

This is the *impossibility theorem* of cultural theory. It points out that the perceptual bias inherent in each of the four social contexts incorporates a distinct moral basis for justification and legitimation. A glance through the rows of Table 5.1 will confirm that each political culture has its own distinctive stabilizing moral basis, and that each would be destabilized if it were to apply to itself any of the biases that stabilize the others. The only way people can shift their cultural premises is by changing the kinds of social constraints that lead them to give credence to a particular set of moral principles, which, of course, will at the same time shift them across into a different quadrant. Conversely, any change in social context (as, for instance, happened to our local objector and our troublesome critic) will trigger commitment to a different package of culturally induced cognitive premises.[9] (Of course, this is not a proof of the impossibility theorem; that is something that is yet to be achieved in cultural theory. What it does do is help confirm that the state of affairs posited by the theorem does indeed exist.[10])

From Individuals as Social Beings to Policy Actors as Aggregations of Individuals

If, for the moment, we assume that cultural theory can be applied not just to individuals and their social contexts but also to policy actors (corporations, government departments, trade unions, local authorities, public interest groups, and so on), then we can analyze the conflicting preferences and justifications that drive the whole decision process in terms of a limited and eternally valid set of ideal-type socio-cognitive orientations – those that are socially viable and justifiable.[11] This prospect is, to put it mildly, tantalizing to policy analysts, who all too often nowadays find themselves vilified by those they are seeking to help for getting their *de*scriptions and their *pre*scriptions hopelessly entangled. A map of all the biases would provide them with a splendidly *de*scriptive base from which those that they are advising could themselves evaluate the options and arrive at their own *pre*scriptions. Everything, therefore, hangs on the initial assumption: that the theory applies to policy actors as well as to individual social beings. Is it, we must now ask, valid?

The transition from the individual to the wider social stage on which he or she acts (from micro to macro, as economists put it) is notoriously difficult, both within neoclassical economics and within the theory of social choice (whose most celebrated theorem, Arrow's theorem, actually proves that, if we start from the assumptions that constitute the individualist fallacy, it is impossible). The strength of the cultural theory, however, is that it sets off by treating individuals not as self-sustaining and diverse bundles of preferences but as social beings; people who, in deriving their individuality from their involvement with others, are already connected up into the wider scheme of things. Consequently, it has no difficulty in conceptualizing social organizations in terms of what are, in effect, aggregations of similarly institutionalized individuals. It is this that enables institutionalized policy actors to be classified by reference to the culturally induced personal strategies, perceptions and justifications of the grid/group map.

Indeed, the very fact that these aggregations can be seen (both by themselves and others) to *be* policy actors tells us that their constituent individuals (far from displaying the gloriously varied preferences stipulated by the individualist fallacy) have already, as the expression so aptly puts it, got their act together. Cultural biases, you could say, align potential constituents who, when conditions are right, effortlessly coalesce into institutional policy actors.

There are, we may conclude, no insuperable obstacles to the use of the political cultures frame in policy analysis. It will, we may expect, be particularly useful in the analysis of policy conflicts since it allows the social and political arena to be conceived of as a strongly patterned process of cultural contention between the basic socio-cognitive orientations of its constituents. In place of the traditional static separation between the political arena and the politics it contains – between frame and framed, goal setting and goal seeking – cultural theory presents us with a dynamic and variegated whole: a self-organizing system that, hitherto, has been extraordinarily inaccessible to us precisely because we are inescapably a part of it. It is by our never-ending contentions that it organizes itself.

This image of systemic self-organization is, perhaps, the most novel and alarming accompaniment of the cultural theory. In suggesting that it is the totality (the contention of the parts) that somehow presses the button on us (so long as we all continue to act in the conviction that it is we who are pressing the button on it) cultural theory has fairly put the cat among the liberal pigeons. At any rate, it looks as though it has; and it is this illiberal appearance, we have found, that is the main obstacle to the theory's easy acceptance.

Obstacles to accepting the cultural theory

There are those who, whilst concurring with this cultural and institutional approach, simply cannot bring themselves to go along with what they see to be the drastic demotion of the individual that it entails. Fearful of the totalitarian excesses that, they believe, will be unleashed by any questioning of the individualist fallacy, they still cling to the tenets of utilitarianism even though they find them to be intellectually untenable. This sophisticated contortion, we would point out, assumes that the human ability to choose between one way of life – one 'grand type' – and another (which is what our cultural theory extends to the social being) is less dignified than being free to choose between one brand of margarine and another, which is what the current theories of rational choice allow him. Another version of the same sophistry is to reject cultural theory on the grounds that it is wrong to put people into boxes, a response that ignores the fact that it is busy putting everyone into just one box, whilst the cultural theory it rejects is allowing people to build the boxes of their choice!

We mention these objections, first, because we have become acutely aware of their prevalence and, second, because that prevalence lends some empirical support to our argument that the cultural edifice we are building will be very different from the familiar politics of interest structure that it replaces. Let us now conclude this chapter by briefly reiterating that new structure in the form appropriate to its application in policy analysis.

The Framework

In the cultural analysis of policy behaviour the operative word is bias, not cause. Cultural analysis provides a scheme that models the variation in cultural selection and institutional choice, rather than being itself explanatory. Provided we can point to justificatory and strategic mechanisms that draw the contexts of some individuals into alignment with one another and set them apart from those of others, the cultural typology can be applied at various levels of aggregation, though not, we must stress, at the level of the society as a whole. That, the cultural theory insists, must always remain disaggregated into its essential biases (Ostrander 1982).

The justificatory and strategic mechanisms that align multitudinous individuals into unitary policy actors are, of course, the different ways of organizing that go with each of the political cultures. Boundary setting and ways of organizing, the theory insists, must match up. If a policy actor's boundary setting – the risks and benefits that are given salience by its perceptual bias, for instance, and its definitions of problem and solution – are not those appropriate to its clearly discernible way of organizing then that actor is, for some reason, using *stolen rhetoric*.

Those who call themselves 'appropriate technologists', for instance, are organized as an egalitarian bounded group and are, the cultural theory predicts, committed to small-scale technology. It is the individualists who are the appropriate technologists, selecting whatever scale offers them the most promising rate of return. Once the stolen rhetoric has been spotted (by its mismatch with the way of organizing of the actor who mouths it) we can move on to examine the deeds that accompany the words; we can look at the technologies that the appropriate technologists are developing and implementing. All, it turns out, are small in scale. Another example of stolen rhetoric is the recent conversion of Ed Teller (the 'father of the H-bomb' and a leading figure in the pro-nuclear and pro-market organization Scientists and Engineers for Secure Energy, SE_2) to environmentalism. Since this conversion has not precipitated his resignation from SE_2, or his espousal of unilateral disarmament, the rhetoric does not match up with his way of organizing. Rather, it is a piece of individualistic opportunism. Coal, it can now be argued, is more environmentally harmful than uranium: come over to the clean fuel! Since we will be encountering more examples of stolen rhetoric in the chapters that follow, it is important that the problems and capabilities it raises be confronted before our analyses begin.

The existence of stolen rhetoric does not undermine the cultural theory. On the contrary; if the different ways of organizing did not already own different rhetorics how could they steal them from one another? Indeed, the very fact that the stolen rhetoric does not match up with the way of organizing of the actor who has stolen it, and that it is actually being used (while the opportunity exists) in the furtherance of that way of organizing, is an impressive vindication of the plural rationalities framework: without it you could not have begun to sort out what was going on. Furthermore, cultural theory shows us that if stolen rhetoric did not exist it would be necessary to invent it. Particular cultural commitments – to one of the dose–response curves, against paradichlorobenzene, to high-rise systems building, against multinationals, and so on – are all historically contingent. They are manifestations of one or other of the myths of nature at a particular time, in a particular place, given the present state of scientific knowledge, and given the present state of technological development. But time, place, science and technology all change, and this means that, if the myths are not to become historically entrained, and so lose their eternal validity, particular commitments will eventually have to be relinquished and new ones taken up. Rhetoric stealing is what makes these essential relinquishments and uptakes possible.

At a more practical level, the existence of stolen rhetoric stresses the importance of looking not just at the varieties of boundary setting – the policy positions and justifications – but at the policy actors' established patterns of social relationships as well. It is these two together (demonstrably depending on one another), and not just a superficial pigeonholing of rhetorics, that cultural analysis must be concerned with.

The ways of organizing

The four stabilizable conjunctions of social context and cultural bias lead (confusingly it would seem) to three distinctive forms of social organization: the ego-focused group, the hierarchically nested group, and the bounded egalitarian group.[12] These are the basic bricks from varying combinations of which all our institutions are put together, and they are sustained by the cognitive biases of the individualist, the hierarchist and the egalitarian, respectively. The fatalist, as one might expect given his passivity, is the squeezed-out residue from these organization-building activities. This both explains the appparent confusion of three organizational forms sustaining four cultural biases and suggests that fatalism will be an essential component in any viable polity. Nor, as we have seen, are these institutional types, for all the strangeness of their grid/group garb, entirely novel. The first two (the individualist and the hierarchist) are in many ways compatible with the twofold classification in terms of markets and hierarchies to which many social theorists (in contravention of the individualist fallacy) have habitually referred. What cultural theory does is to enrich this distinction by revealing the two dimensions of sociality that generate it and then filling in the remaining two types – the fatalists and the egalitarians – that complete the typology.[13]

The upper-right quadrant of the cultural scheme (positive group/positive grid; see Figure 1.2) is the natural environment of highly prescribed institutional action, where group loyalty is rewarded and formal status distinction respected. It belongs to the hierarchy, where every member knows his or her place, securely bounded and unambiguously stratified. Keeping things in their places, transactions in their proper channels, and parts subservient to the whole are the actions that must be fostered if stability is to be achieved. This political culture, therefore, can be characterized as biased towards *ritualism and sacrifice*.

In the diametrically opposite corner of the social context space (negative grid/negative group) individuals have ample freedom for negotiating relationships on the basis of contractual exchanges. This social environment allows for maximum individual mobility up and down whatever the scale of authority or influence. Here one finds the ideal-type free market organization, characterized by the proliferation of ego-focused networks and by entrepreneurial activity aimed at private profit seeking of all kinds. The individualist expands his network in all promising directions; he has no interest in the maintenance of permanent transactional boundaries. The market institution is stabilized by the view that anything is negotiable in the pursuit of personal rewards in a competitive environment. The individualistic political culture is biased towards *pragmatic materialism*.

Since the third institutional type is organized as a bounded egalitarian group (sometimes called a clan, or a club or a sect or an equity), it scores high on the group dimension. Its members are collectively protective against the outside world. It is bound together by a common set of ideals to which all members voluntarily subscribe (think of the Voluntary Simplicity Movement in the United States). It rejects, however, the hierarchy and all the prescriptions and institutionalized inequalities that characterize highly stratified contexts. That is, it scores negatively on the grid dimension. Authority resides not in the individual, nor on the basis of status, but in the collectivity as a whole. The bias of this egalitarian political culture is towards *fundamentalism* (just one vital boundary to protect) and *millenarianism* (the perfect world we will all enter when that boundary no longer has to be protected).

In moving from individual behaviour to the level of institutional behaviour pertinent to public policy making, cultural theory suggests that one of the four cultural strategies will not be actively present in the policy arena.[14] Given the continual pressures upon the fatalist by those subscribing to hierarchical authority, by successful individualistic competitors, and by boundary-maintaining egalitarians, this social type is excluded at the level of institutional interaction. Fatalists find it impossible to involve themselves with lasting, socially viable group or network relations, and are incapable of participating in public policy debates. They have enough on their short-term plates just coping with the vagaries of their unpredictable and uncontrollable environment ('why bother to vote', they will rationalize, 'the government always gets in'). The individual caught up in this positive grid/negative group social context has scope for neither autonomous personal transactions nor group immersion. His behaviour is entirely restricted by the social prescriptions that others have thrust upon him.

Unable to influence social transactions through group membership and incapable of successfully building the entrepreneurial networks required to escape from their prescribed (but not necessarily miserable[15]) fate, fatalists remain peripheral to any stable patterns of organizational interaction. More than that, these patterns actually achieve their stability by the creation and perpetuation of this vast margin. It is for this reason that the fatalists are crucial to policy debates, even though they play no active part in them. Fatalists have to rely on the other institutional types to speak on their behalf (which they do, each in its distinctive way). Alternatively, of course, they can try to migrate to other social contexts. The fatalist's political culture is biased towards an *inconsistent eclecticism*. It is, to those looking down on it from the outside, a kitsch assemblage presided over by Lady Luck.

This fourfold scheme provides us with a methodological grip on the process by which policy actors set boundaries to decision situations. The confrontation of distinctive political cultures in the policy arena can be used to analyze, not only the outcome of the public policy process, but also the kinds of selection criteria and justifications that policy actors adopt. By placing the process of public policy making into its proper social contexts, the cultural approach shows us how it is that decision-making institutions become effective or become paralysed according to whether they enjoy the credibility of their members and constituents. In democratic policy making, governmental authorities (for example) are only able to govern effectively as long as their authority is seen as legitimate (MacLean 1982). Cultural theory (as we will show in Chapter 8) provides us with an analytical framework for investigating the dynamic basis for that legitimacy.

Conflicting political cultures, as manifest in the policy arena, define the basic differences in consent and social support from which policy actors derive the credibility for their choices, as well as for their authority. The political cultures model, therefore, allows us to conceptualize the contention of the distinctive cultural orientations by which policy actors seek to preserve an adequate measure of social consent. It shows us how the arena is constructed, how policy actors are able to climb into it, and what they will then have to do if they are not to be thrown out of it.

Notes

1. For instance, the House of Commons Environment Committee (in its first report, *Radioactive Waste*, 1986) puts it like this:

   > Radiation is for most people inexplicable, unseeable, untouchable, and almost mystically evil in its association with the appalling destructive power of atomic weapons. It is also associated with that other great twentieth century fear, cancer. Most frightening of all are the unknown effects, the genetic changes which might pass on to future generations. It is hardly surprising if the public's view of things nuclear is at times emotional rather than rational.

2. Stephen Cotgrove (1982) also convincingly relates ideas of nature to social formations, although his identification of only two – catastrophists and cornucopians – makes his typology less variegated than the fourfold one we are using.

3. And we may refer here to Schattschneider's widely quoted statement that 'organization is the mobilization of bias' (1960: 71).

4. This, in a very rough sketch, is what Basil Bernstein (1971, 1973, 1975) calls the 'collection curriculum'. Although the two axes – speech codes and control modes – that Bernstein sets up to analyze educational

institutions do not map perfectly onto the axes of cultural theory (one quadrant, for instance, is 'uninhabited'), his work in the sociology of education has been a major influence on that theory's development.

5. Caneva (1981) has discussed the different culturally induced epistemologies in relation to disputes over scientific theories.

6. Strictly speaking, the classification is *five*fold because it is possible, under certain conditions, for individuals to pull back from all four 'engaged' ways of life into a state of withdrawal from all coercive social involvement. This is the *hermit's* way of life; one that is followed by certain individuals in our complex industrial societies and by entire communities in the Himalayas and other margins where power is, for one reason or another, much attentuated.

    Since hermits withdraw from the sorts of sociality that are embraced by the hierarchists, the individualists, the egalitarians and the fatalists, Mary Douglas has elected to 'take them off the social map'. In this book we feel justified in following her lead because the hermit, it seems to us, has little if any influence on the processes by which technologies develop. Those readers who are interested in finding out something of how he fits onto the social map, and of how the communities that are organized around this hermitic ideal achieve viability, should see Thompson (1982a, b) and Thompson and Wildavsky (1986b).

7. Mary Douglas, who uses grid/group as just an analytical framework, has the axes running from 0 to 1 (or from 'weak' to 'strong'). However, since we are using these dimensions as part of a theory, we have the axes running from −1 to +1, crossing one another at the origin. This is because we wish to get at the dynamics that must underlie all the organizing and disorganizing. Being prescribed, we note, implies that someone somewhere else is prescribing. And including some people in your group, we note, implies excluding others. Patterns are achieved as much by what they cut out as by what they keep in, and it is the patterns – their possibility and the conditions that have to be satisfied if they are to persist – that we are interested in. The argument for the axes being crossed in this way, and for the hermit being located at the origin, is set out in Thompson (1982a).

8. Except, of course, for the hermit; see notes 6 and 7 above.

9. The 'tipping mechanisms' by which these transitions are effected are explored in Thompson and Tayler (1986).

10. It would be more correct to say that the proof of the impossibility theorem has not yet been given adequate attention. Schmutzer and Bandler (1980) have proved that transaction patterns can only take five forms (their 'trivial' solution, in which no transactions are possible, comporting with the hermit's way of life, the others comporting with

the fourfold predictions we are developing here). They further prove that these five patterns are 'truly distinct types that cannot be transformed into each other unless the principal conditions are altered'.

11. We say *ideal* type because the cultural theory does not require that people always and everywhere act and justify their actions in terms of the strategies and moral frameworks appropriate to the quadrants they occupy. Rather, these quadrants define biases (that is, non-randomnesses or tendencies) and all that the cultural theory insists on is that an institution that does not manage to get enough of its constituent individuals to behave and to justify their behaviour in its ideal way, enough of the time, will soon cease to exist. *Genericity* (to use the technical terminology of dynamical systems theory) not total compliance, is what the theory predicts.

12. This dynamical scheme, in which each of these three ways of organizing is busy disorganizing the other two (Thompson 1983a), goes beyond the traditional treatment of culture within organization theory. It subsumes the two main, and seemingly contradictory, perspectives in research on organizational culture to date: the approach that considers culture as an organizational variable (something the organization *has*) and the view that culture is something the organization *is* (Smircich 1983, Riley 1983).

13. The claim that, in addition to the well established twofold typology of markets and hierarchies, a third distinct type of social organization is also viable and necessary has to some extent been vindicated by recent work in sociological and organization theory work concerned with institutions. For example, a third organizational form has been argued, both in contrast to the Weberian rational–bureaucratic model and as an advance on the transactional model of markets and hierarchies (Rothschild-Whitt 1979, Francis *et al.* 1983, Ouchi 1980, Williamson 1973, Williamson and Ouchi 1983). What these types lack, and what cultural theory provides, is a set of social dimensions from which a proper typology can be generated.

14. The hermit, at the centre of the social context map, is of course also absent from serious participation in institutional interaction, since this is a deliberate part of his autonomous strategy. The hermit, by definition, isolates himself from both the processes of group dynamics and the imposition of prescriptions on himself or on others (Thompson 1982a, Douglas 1978).

15. Of all the cultural biases, that of the fatalist is the least well understood. Such descriptions as we have tend to be of how fatalists appear from one or other of the remaining three biases. The hierarchists see them as deviants, the individualists see them as unmotivated, and the

egalitarians see them as downtrodden. How they actually make a life for themselves within all these constraints is a question that has scarcely been addressed by social scientists (Thompson and Wildavsky 1986b). A journalist, however, has made good this omission (Sheehan 1975).

Chapter 6

Among the Energy Tribes

The anthropologist, long used to working among distant and preliterate tribes, has devoted much of his effort to the study of what is called 'the oral tradition'. So it is hardly surprising that, when he finds himself a participant observer in the energy debate, he should try to find his bearings by reference to its oral tradition. When the women and children, the young men and the not-so-young men, gather around the fire and listen to the tales of old men what do they hear?

At the International Institute for Applied Systems Analysis (IIASA) tenure is unknown and the average stay is something less than seven months. This means that even the memories of its most grizzled elders extend only a few years back into the past. Beyond that fuzzy four- or five-year point all is 'dreamtime': a realm of wondrous happenings that are remembered not because they really happened (though they may have) but because they have some crucial significance for the present.

The start of the IIASA Energy Project, back in 1972, is lost in this dreamtime, and one of the tales that is sometimes recounted to the young warrior scientists concerns an heroic encounter between the Great Energy Chief and the Divine Trickster (disguised, on this occasion, as a visiting economist).

The Great Energy Chief drew on the blackboard a little diagram of The Problem. Energy demand was increasing but energy supply was beginning to fall away. An energy gap had already opened up and, if nothing was done about it, it would go on getting worse and worse. The solution lay in somehow or other increasing supply so as to close the ever-widening gap (see Figure 6.1).

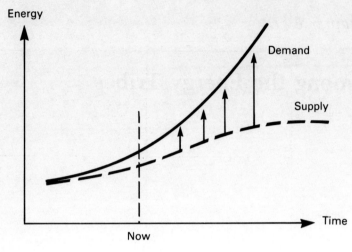

Figure 6.1

The Divine Trickster then stood up and said that the economist would see this as only one, rather extreme, solution within a whole range of possible solutions. The supply and demand curves were linked by the price mechanism, and their reconciliation would depend on such things as the elasticity of supply and the elasticity of demand; things that, to some greater or lesser extent, might be influenced by policy.

'Ah yes', said the Great Energy Chief, 'but economics is a soft science and we are taking a hard science approach to The Problem.'

At this the Divine Trickster went up to the blackboard and drew a square that, so the assembled multitude thought, he would presently fill with complex details of the price mechanism. But no; he turned it into a 2 x 2 matrix, labelled its rows and columns, and then, muttering something about 'no names, no pack-drill', returned to his chair (Figure 6.2).

Hard science, the hard scientists tell us, is value-free. It is the soft sciences – psychology, economics, anthropology – that are value-laden and, in consequence, find themselves tossed this way and that as (to use the Great Energy Chief's own words) 'perceptions and preferences . . . change with new information, new propaganda and new paradigms for viewing the human experience' (Häfele 1981:26).

If we accept this hard/soft distinction (and, with certain provisos, we are prepared to do that) we still need to think about what will happen when the hard scientist gets to work on something – the

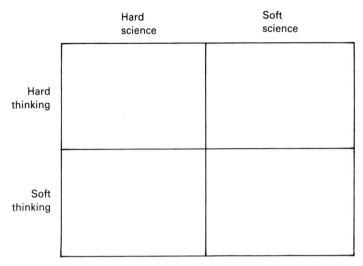

Figure 6.2

world's energy future – that, of its very nature, is value-laden. It is the Great Energy Chief's failure to do that piece of 'hard thinking' that the Divine Trickster has so charmingly put his finger on.

Although the International Institute for Applied Systems Analysis may sound like a satirist's invention, it is a real place; we have worked there. It is housed in a Habsburg palace at Laxenburg, just outside Vienna, and scientists from East and West come there to work on problems of common interest. Energy is very much one of those problems, and the IIASA Energy Project has been the institute's largest single undertaking to date. More than 250 scientists worked on this project, tens of millions of dollars were spent on it, and the central feature of its vast and authoritative final report, *Energy in a Finite World*, was the set of three enormous computer models that, when linked together into an iterative loop, generated scenarios that indicated the sorts of directions in which the world's energy future could go (Figure 6.3).

The project was endorsed by the Max Planck Society, the American Academy of Sciences, the Soviet Academy of Sciences, the Royal Society of London, and a host of other prestigious organizations. What is more, several countries (the Soviet Union, West Germany and the United Kingdom among them) relied heavily on this report in formulating and justifying their national energy policies.

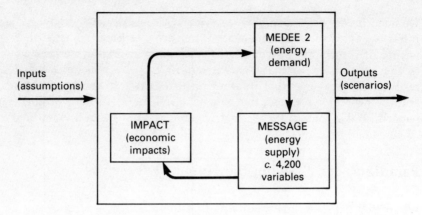

Figure 6.3 The IIASA energy models.

One of us, working day after day in close proximity to this Energy Project, began to feel that, far from having its feet firmly on the ground (which is what the hard scientists who manned it insisted), it was a wonderfully complex and free-floating elaboration of just one of those 'paradigms for viewing the human experience' to which its final report so disparagingly refers. He wrote a working paper to this effect (Thompson 1982a) which, since it was couched in the language of soft science, failed to capture the attention of the members of the project and later was able to get together with a sociologist of science (Brian Wynne) and a mathematician (Bill Keepin) to investigate these suspicions more fully.

To cut a long and at times murky story short, Keepin was eventually able to demonstrate, in the hardest of mathematical language, that these suspicions were well-founded. His technique was to simplify the models (which contained on the order of 4,200 variables each) by throwing away variables and seeing if that made any difference to the output, the energy scenarios. If it did, then the variable had to be put back, if it did not, then it could be discarded. Eventually, he was able to throw *all* the variables away, and to show that the outputs (the scenarios) were 'hard-wired' to the inputs (the far from explicit assumptions that had, in fact, provided the cultural cohesion for the project). The results of this little piece of quality control within the Institute were eventually published in *Nature* (Keepin and Wynne 1984) and, at greater length, in a special issue of the journal *Policy Sciences* (Keepin *et al.*, 1984). The consequences, we need hardly say, have been profound. More than anything else, it has been this sequence of events – the demonstration of the hard-wiring of scenarios to assumptions, the obstacles that were raised to the publication of that demonstration, and the brouhaha that resulted from its eventual publication – that has transformed the anthropological hypothesis that was advanced in the initial working paper into the cultural theory that we are expounding in this book.

Paradigms for Viewing the Human Experience

When the hard scientist maintains that the paradigms for viewing the human experience are always changing, and that this makes the study of perception 'a very soft science indeed' (Häfele 1981:26), the cultural hypothesis asserts the exact opposite: that these paradigms are immutable, small in number, and quite easily described. The key to that description is provided by the four myths of nature that continually resurface through the turbulent contingencies of history to reassert their essential timelessness. Three of these myths do their resurfacing in the policy arena; indeed, that is what actually creates and endlessly recreates that arena. So we took the published material relating to the energy debate – its written tradition – and searched through that 'universe', as best we could, for clear evidence of distinct, mutually contradictory, and threefold perceptions of the problem.[1] We then went on to see whether these sets of contradictory certainties correlated, first, with the hypothesized political cultures and, second, with one another.

We found five descriptions that satisfied these requirements (since then, another one (Spronk and Veeneklass 1983) has come to our attention). The way in which they matched up with the predictions of the hypothesis, and with one another, is rendered all the more remarkable by the fact that not one of these accounts refers to any of the others. They seem to have been arrived at independently and without any of the convergent pressures of mutual awareness.

Harman et al. (1977)

These authors are engineers with a particular interest in the harness-ing of solar energy. Long immersed in energy matters (and sensitized, perhaps, by their solar zeal to the responses of their fellow engineers) they have come to discern three distinct perceptions, A, B and C. They characterize these perceptions by a quite extensive list of tripartite distinctions, many of which are also picked up in the other tripartite descriptions that we have looked at. If we summarize these characterizations in terms of problem and solution definitions – the different, and contradictory, ways in which energy demand and supply are perceived as being reconciled – we get something like this.

- *Perception A*: 'Onward and upward'. The present trend, given our present skills and knowledge, is sustainable (and, of course, desirable).
- *Perception B*: 'Gradual smooth descent'. The present trend is (with some regrets) not sustainable and the solution lies in an orderly transition (carefully planned so as to minimize social and economic disruption) to a sustainable future.
- *Perception C*: 'Sudden discontinuous descent'. The present trend is (no regrets) not sustainable and the solution – a sustainable future – can only be reached by a radical change now: a change that will inevitably be accompanied by (desirable) social and economic transformations.

Harman *et al.* provide a persuasive description which they buttress, to good effect, with arguments borrowed from the history of science (Thomas Kuhn) and from anthropology (Ruth Benedict), but they do not seek an explanation. Rather, their attitude is that these three perceptions are facts of life and, instead of asking 'where do they come from?' and 'how can we get rid of them?', their concern is with the much more practical and policy-relevant question 'how do we live with them?'.

They argue that these perceptions are just *there* and that it would be wildly optimistic to assume that two of them will presently go away and leave us with a single outright winner. Furthermore, these perceptions all lie within the bounds of expert credibility, not in the sense that energy experts of one persuasion concede the expertise of those of the other two persuasions (though they sometimes may), but in the sense that the socially conferred label 'expert' is at present attached to some individuals of each persuasion. This means that we simply cannot give an answer to the question 'which perception is the right one?'. They conclude that, when there is such persistent disagreement among both experts and lay people, the adversary mode (arguing about which perception is right) becomes counterproductive as a way of deciding policy. Instead, they urge an exploratory mode (discovering where and when each perception is appropriate) and, without too much discussion of what this might be, they point out that if we are to move to such a mode we must, somehow or other, legitimate all these perceptions.

Schanz (1978)

Whereas Harman *et al.* are concerned with energy in general, Schanz zeroes in on just two energy sources, oil and gas, and we might be excused for expecting that, within the specific confines and technicalities of this particular field, there would be little scope for expert disagreement. But no; the microcosm of oil and gas perfectly reproduces the three divergent perceptions of Harman's macrocosm. Schanz, who as a fellow at Resources for the Future has made a detailed historical study of oil and gas reserves estimation in the United States, discerns three distinct 'resource estimates' – those of the optimist, the moderate and the conservative – tightly clumped and widely spaced within an impressively broad sweep of uncertainty. Indeed, this sweep is so broad and has been so resistant, over more than half a century, to all the efforts directed at narrowing it that the history of oil and gas reserves estimation provides a telling indictment of the adversary mode. Since the uncertainty bounds have steadfastly refused to budge, and since the three clearly defined positions within those bounds have always been occupied and resolutely defended, all the money and effort would have been better spent in trying to understand the three positions rather than in a fruitless attempt to find out which one was the right one. For, as all the protagonists would have to concede, the only way you can know how much oil and gas is down there is to get it up here, in which case, of course, it is no longer down there. Perhaps, when it becomes evident that only history will answer a particular question to which we would dearly like to have the answer, that is a signal that we should switch from the adversary to the exploratory mode.

Schanz presents his three resource estimates in the form of a graph plotting the rate of production against time. Up to now, of course, there is only one graph – the historical answer – but, beyond now, any number of graphs are possible (the only constraint being that, at some point, the rates must peak and then decline to world hydrocarbon exhaustion[2]). Out of this vast range of possible graphs just three end up with experts attached to them. Attached to the optimist's graph we find the reservoir engineer, attached to the widely divergent conservative's graph we find the economist, and attached to the moderate's graph (that roughly consistent with averaging these first two) we find the government bureaucrat (Figure 6.4).

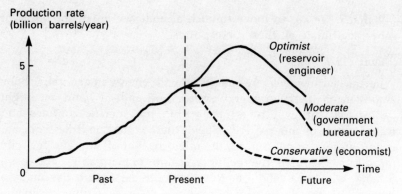

Figure 6.4 Alternative futures for US oil production (after Schanz 1978).

Schanz suggests that the reservoir engineer, long acculturated to a world of exploration and high technology, tends to perceive reserves as bumping up against what is discoverable and recoverable. The economist, on the other hand, sees all things as discoverable and recoverable at a price and he is led, via comparisons with other energy sources, to estimates of what is economically discoverable and recoverable.

The reservoir engineer, with his optimism, his ready acceptance of the high risks of exploration and his faith in technology, lines up nicely with Harman's perception A (and with the individualist in the cultural framework) but what of the economist? It would surely be nonsense to claim that economists are all equipped with perception C and that they are all committed to no-growth and to imminent and radical social change. Whilst some economists (Schumacher 1973 and Georgescu-Roegen 1974, for instance) might fit the bill, any theory that tried to put Milton Friedman (say) or Friedrich Hayek among the Cs could scarcely be said to have reduced the arbitrariness of description. No, Schanz's economist is not saying that energy demand will have to fall but that the time is coming when other energy sources will have to be substituted for oil and gas. Only those economists who argue that these other energy sources too are all subject to the same sort of pessimistic constraints are aligning themselves with Harman's perception C.

Taxation rates (and tax exemptions) for the oil companies will, of course, have the effect of modifying the constraints that bear upon the reservoir engineer and, in much the same way, price regulation will lessen or exacerbate the constraints that the economist sees as Friedrich Hayek among the Cs could scarcely be said to have reduced paramount. In wielding these instruments the government bureaucrat has no interest in being more optimistic than the reservoir engineer or more pessimistic than the economist because if he chose either of these two extreme options he would, in effect, be handing over control entirely to one or other of these perceptions, and the government bureaucrat's aim is not to hand over control but to maximize it. If his control decreases the nearer he gets to one or other extreme then it must increase the farther he gets away from them both and, since to put himself beyond either extreme would automatically result in his total loss of control, the best he can do is to steer a course between, but roughly equidistant from, them both.

Once government has intervened, by regulating prices and by instituting tax incentives or disincentives for exploration, then strategic behaviour and stolen rhetoric begins to cloud the picture as the savage beast of capitalism sees, from time to time, the advantage of concealing his entrepreneurial spots and pretending that one of the other resource estimates is the correct one.[3] In this way, the history of energy reserves estimation (the data that the government insists on collecting as the basis for its interventions) becomes a *roman à clef* within which the strategizing actors are continually changing their names and their styles of dress.[4] But the key – the only way of disentangling this convoluted charade – is provided by the three active cultural biases for, only if they pre-exist, as immutable perceptual bases, is it possible for the strategizing actors to hop, this way and that, between them.

This mobility, of course, is possible only because oil and gas constitute but a part of the energy whole. If Schanz's three resource estimates applied right across the energy board then an individual with a particular perception would have to stick with the appropriate resource estimate; but they do not apply right across the board and this means that, depending on what he sees happening with other energy sources, an individual can hop about from one base to another yet still remain perceptually consistent. American oil companies have, over the years, become so agile that many American motorists, even as they waited bumper-to-bumper in the gas lines (petrol queues in Britain), simply refused to believe that there was an oil crisis in 1979 and saw it instead as a situation that had been deliberately engineered by the oil companies in order to force government to allow prices to rise, thereby increasing the oil companies' profits.

When experts disagree we might expect that, as good scientists, their resource estimates would be somewhat randomly spread out between the uncertainty bounds. Certainly, one would not expect them to be gathered together like three droplets of mercury on a flat surface. Yet this is what seems to be happening. Uncertainty, by definition, is unpredictable but reaction to uncertainty, though it can take a number of widely divergent forms, would appear to be so strongly patterned – so predictable – as to be almost certain. This surprising orderliness in the reaction to uncertainty calls for some explanation, and one plausible explanation is that some resource estimates are specially privileged because they justify some policy or other. If you assume that policies, like plots in literature, are few and far between then tightly clumped and widely spaced resource estimates, far from causing surprise, are what you would expect to see. The interesting question then becomes, 'what leads one individual to support one policy (and to give credence to one estimate) and another individual to support another policy (and to give credence to a different estimate)?'. The conventional answer, of course, is 'self-interest', and both the clumps and the pattern of recruitment to them simply serve to confirm (to those who are interested in pushing the explanation this far) the existing arrangement of social control over the means of production at any particular historical moment. Such an explanation is essentially an explanation in terms of goal-seeking and, whilst not necessarily disagreeing with it, we should try to shift the whole discussion onto a less trivial plane and ask how the goals that people seek are set. But, first, let us complete the case for the clumps.

In the history of oil and gas reserves estimation it is the three cultural biases that provide *la clef* whilst it is the part–whole relationship between oil/gas and energy that makes *le roman* (the strategizing behaviour of the characters) possible. This means that, if we want to get hold of the key, we must first put a stop to the strategizing – to all the name changing, hat swapping and rhetoric stealing as the various characters opportunely hop this way and that between the widely spaced positions. This we can do by insisting (for a moment) that the resource estimates for oil and gas also apply across the whole energy board. If we do this, what policies do these three estimates justify?

- *The optimist's:* The trend, for the time being at least, is a continuation of the recent past. Of course, there will be a downturn in the longer term, but if you have faith in the ingenuity of future generations and so are prepared to discount the future, then it is business as usual.
- *The conservative's:* We are now *at* the turning point. From now

on the future will be altogether different from the present and the past. If we persist on our present path then we will inevitably be using up the energy birthright of future generations. To the extent that we delay the downturn we will simply be making it steeper and, indeed, at a not-too-far-distant point it will actually become vertical and, after that, we simply will not be able to reach a sustainable future – we will have spent it all. The message is clear: radical change now, before it is too late.

- *The moderate's*: We are not yet at the turning point but it is coming and, if we are to successfully adapt to the downturn, we will have to start making our preparations now. We simply cannot go on doing as we have been doing; there will have to be change. But it would be wrong to try to make the changes that are necessary all at once, now. Rather, the answer lies in an orderly, gradual and carefully planned transition that will bring us safely to a sustainable future with the minimum of economic dislocation and social confusion. The optimist and the conservative may see this as a middle-of-the-road policy but that is because the one is obsessed with the short term and the other is over-reacting to the long term.

Clearly, there is more to these three policies than the purely technical weighing of expert arguments as to how we should best arrange the ways in which we supply our society with energy. These policies do not just take society as a given – they have serious implications for it. Depending upon which policy you choose, you will move towards one or other of these alternative social arrangements. Here then, in the social implications of energy policy, is the clue to why some people give credibility to one perception and other people to other perceptions. All we have to do is reverse the priority of policy and social implication. If resource estimates are clumped in order to provide justifications for energy policies then energy policies are best understood as arguments for ways of life, as rationalizations for different kinds of desired social arrangements.

If this is the case then the conventional sequence will have to be reversed. In this sequence you first establish the facts (how much is down there) and then, on the basis of those facts, deduce a number of feasible policies from which, by a process of careful evaluation (which includes some weighing of the social implications of these policies), you finally select the best. Instead, you start with a socially induced predilection that leads you to favour the sort of social arrangements promised by one policy and to disfavour those promised by the alternative policies. Having chosen your policy you then look around for justifications for it and fortunately, thanks to the very wide uncertainty bounds, these are not too difficult to come by. With the help of just a few large and largely unquestioned assumptions about how the world is, you can come up with a hard science estimate of how much is down there that will clearly demonstrate that your chosen policy is far and away the best (perhaps, even, the only) one available.

Chapman (1975)

Whereas Schanz has looked at one energy source in the United States, Chapman has looked at energy across the board in Britain and has arrived at a very similar typology. Indeed, after Harman and Schanz, there is something rather *déjà vu* about Chapman's three energy futures ('business as usual', 'technical fix' and 'low growth') and his typology meshes so smoothly with those from across the Atlantic as to cast serious doubt on the sort of dismissive response that sees all these perceptual excesses as unique to California.

Schanz has pointed out that, in resource estimation, there is nothing that can be measured and that, in consequence, the whole business is inevitably judgemental and subjective (he compares it to 'going to an unfamiliar supermarket on a foggy night and trying to estimate the total amount of asphalt used in paving the parking lot, with no other data than a cubic inch sample of the blacktop used'). Inevitably, those who make the resource estimates are 'projecting past experience into the future' (Schanz 1978:10). But what happens if we reverse Schanz's causal logic and say that they are projecting the future into past experience? One thing that happens is that we substitute a final cause for an efficient cause; not in the sense that something that is going to happen in the future has caused something to happen in the past but in the sense that, within the bounds of uncertainty that are available to us, we interpret the past in terms of a future that our imagination (and our myths) has already put 'out there' for us. The essential point is that what we do today largely depends on how we interpret the past, and our interpretation of the past will, to a considerable extent, be shaped by the futures that our desires have already created. And if, as hard scientists, we cannot (try as we may) discover how much there is down there, at least, as soft scientists, we can say something about the conflicting desires – the myths – that exist up here.

To do this we need to reverse Schanz's second temporal conclusion: that 'the choice of the type of curve to be used preordains in a general way what the future will look like' (Schanz 1978:9). Instead, we should conclude that the choice of future preordains in a general way the type of curve to be used (think of the three dose–response curves). What happens when we approach Chapman's three energy futures from this imaginative and contrary direction?

If these three energy futures are already 'out there' as final causes – as fixed points which, somehow or other, we have to home-in on – then it should be possible, by looking at these homing-in requirements, to isolate just what it is that distinguishes the three paradigms and maintains their separation.

- *The individualist*: 'Business as usual'. This energy future lies out there on the extrapolation of the recent trend. To get to it we have to carry on as we have been doing, innovating with skill and confidence – no easy matter when all around us Jeremiahs insist that it cannot be done.
- *The hierarchist*: 'Technical fix'. The future is different from the present but it does not press too closely upon us. This gap between the future out there and our present trajectory, though a blessing in many ways, creates some navigational problems that are unique to this future.
- *The egalitarian*: 'Low growth'. The future is altogether different from the present and, at the same time, it is so close that we can only reach it by a sudden switch, like an electron jumping from one orbit to another.

In the individualist faith, as long as you keep up the present innovation-fuelled momentum you will arrive at the business as usual future; in the egalitarian faith, once you have committed yourself to your quantum jump you are bound to find yourself in the new low-growth orbit (but you have to jump now: he who hesitates is lost). But to reach the technical fix future you have to walk a social and economic tightrope and, before you walk this tightrope you have to erect it. So, in the hierarchical faith, the tightrope (the plan for the transition) and the walking of the tightrope (the successful implementation of that plan) become the paramount concerns. And, of course, tightrope walkers soon develop superb balance and quickly learn to avoid any sudden jerky movements (Figure 6.5).

Two qualitative criteria (whether the future is the continuation of the present and whether there is a time gap between the future and

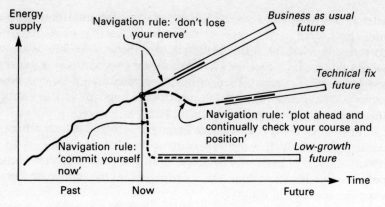

Figure 6.5 The three futures and how to reach them.

	Is future a continuation of the present?	Is there a time gap between future and present?
Business as usual	Yes	No
Technical fix	No	Yes
No growth	No	No

Figure 6.6 Criteria for separating the three futures.[5]

the present) are sufficient to separate and define these three futures (Figure 6.6).

Humphrey and Buttel (1980); Orr (1977)

Since both these tripartite descriptions are drawn from a political science perspective, they can be taken together. Humphrey's and Buttel's interest is in the growth/no-growth debate – with the entire environmental question rather than specifically with energy – and they neatly reverse the whole framework to show that social scientists, too, are only human and that they have three paradigms just like everyone else. Humphrey and Buttel label these social science paradigms the conservative, the liberal and the radical and, after listing the way in which they are distinguished by different ideas of culture, power and stratification, they go on to outline the sorts of policies that those who subscribe to these different paradigms would be likely to advocate. Even though they provide little that is specific to the energy debate, their three paradigms line up with those of Harman *et al.*, Schanz and Chapman (and of the cultural theory) without any difficulty (apart, that is, from such superficial confusions as their conservative lining up with the individualist, while Schanz's conservative lines up with the egalitarian).

Orr, on the other hand, addresses himself squarely to energy policy and identifies three distinct 'perspectives' which he labels supply, conservation and energetics. These labels he derives from the different ways in which the problem is defined. From the supply perspective the problem is inadequate energy supply (the same problem as that which beset the Great Energy Chief); from the conservation perspective it is, rather, the problem of energy waste; and from the energetics perspective it is essentially a cultural and social problem. The reason people see the problem differently, Orr goes on to argue, is that they start with different assumptions and these, again, line up nicely with the three active cultural biases. In the supply perspective energy and economic growth are assumed to be coupled and energy growth is assumed to continue. In the conservation perspective it is assumed that energy and economic growth can be decoupled,[6] enabling the economy to go on growing while energy growth is slowed. In the energetics perspective energy growth and economic growth are assumed to be coupled but our present path flies in the face of the laws of thermodynamics and cannot continue. Cheap energy is a thing of the past.

Embedded in these assumptions about what is and is not possible are three very different ideas of how the world is, how it works, and how man fits into it; it would be nice to know what kind of social being is led to each set of assumptions and how. Orr does this by listing the primary actors (together with the sorts of governance they see as desirable) and by listing the energy goals (together with their implications for social values) towards which these primary actors aspire. In the supply perspective the primary actors (Orr is only concerned with the United States) are the energy corporations, and they would prefer to operate in a *laissez-faire* world with a minimum of government intervention. Their goal is inexhaustible cheap energy, a goal that entails 'no value change'.

In the conservation perspective the primary actor is 'government' and the desired operating milieu one in which government plays a major role: 'Leviathan'. Significantly, in view of the hierarchist's distinction between the future 'out there' and the getting to it, Orr lists two goals for his Leviathan: a near-term goal of efficiency (conservation and decoupling) and a long-term goal of inexhaustible (but not necessarily cheap) energy supply. To reach these goals there will have to be a 'small value change'. In the energetics perspective the primary actor is 'the public'. (We have to differ with Orr at this point. Only if his three perspectives were exhaustive, only if everyone in the society had a speaking part in the energy policy play, would it be correct to call this primary actor 'the public'. Since we maintain that there is another perspective, the fatalist's, that never participates, we would have to redefine Orr's 'public' as 'those who credibly claim to speak with the authentic voice of the people'.) This primary actor, not surprisingly, wishes to participate; to blow the whistle on government; and to reaffirm a Jeffersonian style of governance. This actor's goal is a decentralized, solar-based society, a goal that requires a 'radical value change'.

Orr then goes on to deduce the different sorts of risks that loom largest in each perspective: economic disruption in the supply perspective; balance of payments, overseas dependence and energy wars in the conservation perspective; technological accidents, resource exhaustion and climate change in the energetics perspective. Only after he has done this – only after he has listed the three definitions of the problem, the three sets of assumptions, the three primary actors and their desired styles of governance, the three goals and their value implications . . ., the three sets of salient risks – does he leave the social and political arena and enter the world of energy. Almost as an afterthought, the three 'ultimate energy sources' drop out of the bottom of Orr's scheme: breeder/fusion in the supply perspective; conservation technology in the near term leading to breeder/fusion in the long term in the conservation perspective; decentralized solar, wind and biomass in the energetics perspective.

Is There Anything that Stays the Same?

Anyone with even a passing awareness of the energy debate will find much in what we have just described redolent with period charm. The IIASA Energy Project, for instance, was suffused with a touching 1960s faith in the ability of scientists, mathematicians and computers to define and solve all our problems, once and for all.

There was a kind of innocence abroad in the early years of the debate, an innocence that was to be rudely shattered (for the individualists) by OPEC (for the hierarchists), by Three Mile Island and Chernobyl, and (for the egalitarians) by the recent return of something that it was thought had gone for ever – cheap oil. And the three energy technologies that drop so neatly out of Orr's scheme, for all the wisdom that that scheme distils, are already beginning to look rather dated.

The trouble, of course, is that technologies are never irrevocably tied to ways of life, to political cultures and the perceptions and certainties they bring with them. Nor do they ever pop out, fully formed, in this way. Their birth, as the lavatory rim-blocks story makes abundantly clear, is a much messier business; not really a birth at all. Rather, it is a scruffy and incremental *process*; one in which technological developments (never whole technologies) are somehow hammered out between the ways of life that, having made their distinctive technological commitments, manage, as the flux of events carries them along and as they steal a bit of rhetoric from here and have some of their own rhetoric stolen from there, to divest themselves of those commitments that have outlived their usefulness and to attach themselves to new possibilities that (for the moment, at least) better satisfy their eternal criteria.

This is our definition of technology, and it is a definition that raises a host of questions about what, if anything, we can do to influence this ill-formed process of which we are so much a part. How can we assess technology? How can we live with, and make the most of, the contradictory certainties that it entails? How can we ever know which, out of all the technological risks that are perceived, are the ones we should be paying attention to? How can we interpret a historically entrained sequence of physical events and institutional commitments in terms of the eternal and timeless myths that underlie it? How, in other words, do we analyze the inchoate? The first essential, as we stressed in Chapter 1, is to recognize it.

If anything is inchoate it is energy futures. The greenhouse effect, acid rain, somatic and genetic effects of ionizing radiation, the physical and chemical stability of rocks and ocean sediments, the planetary endowment of fossil and other fuels, the longevity of human institutions (which must guard nuclear wastes for millennia), the trajectory of future technical development and public reaction to it, the future energy use of Western and non-Western consumers – all are characterized by complex inter-relationships among multiple variables.

In the mid-1970s, we can now see, there was a brief period of consensus about these matters. Most relevant institutions and experts agreed that ever-increasing demand was exhausting a limited fossil fuel endowment. The longer-term solution to this 'crisis' was clear: a new supply regime based on practically infinite fusion and solar energy. The problem, therefore, was one of transition: how to develop new sources of supply so that economic growth would not falter. The solution was the large-scale development of nuclear power and coal. This required national energy planning, giant public and private sector corporations to finance the necessary investment, and sacrifices by parts of society for the benefit of the whole (sacrifices which included reduced environmental protection and nuclear power plants in many a backyard).

During the course of the 1970s and early 1980s it became clear that this orthodoxy was seriously inaccurate. Not only did events fail to conform to the predictions – energy usage proved more fluid than imagined, energy supply more resilient – the intellectual foundations too proved to be flawed. These flaws were revealed by, *inter alia*, the work on the IIASA energy models and on the estimation of oil and gas reserves that we have just described. Orthodoxy, it became clear, was the hierarchical approach to energy matters. As if by magic, the way it defined the problem, and the solutions it proposed, necessitated large-scale technologies, complex organizations, centralized coordination and great quantities of expertise – in short, more hierarchy. It was increasingly challenged by an egalitarian, or Green, critique which argued that both resource depletion and environmental vulnerability limited energy production and therefore necessitated major cutbacks in energy supply and a rapid transition to renewable energy (thought to be an inherently decentralized energy source). Naturally this required change towards a smaller-scale society, with minimized dependence on external agencies – remote, bureaucratic utilities were regarded with particular contempt – and reduced material prosperity (and, consequently, reduced polarities of wealth). The market rationality challenged both orthodox and Green views of crisis. The benignity of nature meant that resource availability was not a problem; the only constraint was that of human ingenuity in finding new solutions to perennial problems. OPEC could be beaten by unleashing the individualists and allowing market forces both to squeeze energy demand and to encourage new sources of supply.

Each of these interpretations has been both confirmed and refuted by post-1973 experience. New hydrocarbon discoveries and falling oil prices have at least temporarily vindicated the market faith, although the evidence is not sufficiently powerful for orthodox or Green fears of resource scarcity or depletion to be dismissed. The successful French drive towards a nuclear economy apparently validates the orthodox belief in nuclear power, but countries such as Sweden seem to be managing equally well without this technology. The serious environmental problems associated with coal also support the Green critique, but new 'clean coal' technologies may swing the balance towards the orthodox and market perspectives. Renewable energy progress in the last decade has been sufficient to show that the radical ecologist's faith is not completely unfounded; but limited funding and many cogent orthodox arguments against its widespread use still leave its ultimate importance an open question.

The picture remains similarly mixed on environmental matters. 'Spaceship Earth' has had a greater resilience than egalitarians predicted in the 1970s, and the orthodox and individualist faith in the stability of the biosphere has not been shown to be inherently unreasonable. But acid rain, atmospheric carbon dioxide and other global energy-related problems could still turn out to be the qualitatively different environmental perturbations that could send the ball over the edge and create a new, and disastrous, system state.

We can, therefore, see how each of the political cultures has areas that it perceives more clearly than the others, and blind spots where it is unable to see at all. If there were no egalitarians, for example, it is unlikely that renewable energy would have developed in the way it has. If individualists had not been able to explore for oil that those who subscribed to the other political cultures claimed could never exist, many Alaskan and North Sea oil and gas fields might never have been discovered. While the anarchic way that the rationalities have hitherto interacted can no doubt be improved upon, one thing is clear: diversity of conviction can produce major social benefits.

Sliding the Cultural Frame Beneath the Debate

The charm of the energy debate is that it has now gone on long enough to come full circle or, rather, full spiral. Although we have had to break into it at a particular point – the technocratic 1960s – we can now stand back a little and see it for what it is: an endless process which, though it never settles down, and never eradicates the contradictory certainties that drive it, does have a certain, if erratic, rhythm. This rhythm is perhaps best seen as a sort of alternation by the individualists between aligning themselves with the hierarchists or with the hierarchists' radical critics. Offer any new technological development up to the hierarchical or egalitarian criteria and, if it is supported by the one, it will be castigated by the other. But individualists see these entrenched positions, and the momenta they develop, as a rich source of opportunities. In climbing onto the orthodox bandwagon as it gathers momentum, and in jumping off it as it begins to falter, they impart a cyclical pattern to the totality (and in the background, of course, a silent chorus of fatalists endlessly picks up the pieces).

But it is not some nicely disciplined sine curve. Things can get stuck at the top or the bottom, institutionally entrenched technologies can carry it off up blind alleys that then have to be reversed out of at great cost, resources can be committed to carrying it somewhere it could never go or, conversely, to steering it somewhere it was going to go anyway. These wastefulnesses are the sorts of things we may be able to do something about, now that we have some understanding of their dynamics. Taming the whole cycle, however, would be something else.

Since it is the political cultures that provide us with the means of analyzing this process we should now pause, for a moment, to consider their epistemological status. Each, clearly, embodies what the philosopher, Nelson Goodman (1978), has called a *way of worldmaking*. Although he insists that we make the worlds we live in, he also insists that they cannot be just anything we want them to be. The relativism, in other words, is severely constrained, both by culture and by nature. Our cultural theory, by showing how ways of seeing and knowing are always closely linked to ways of organizing, explains how the first of these two sets of constraints arises. The surprises, which the technological trajectories that go with each of the three active ways of worldmaking then run into, are the visible indications of the second set of constraints – the natural ones. Of course, we can never know what all these natural constraints are (we can never anticipate everything) but we can be sure that we will run into them, sooner or later, and that, when we do, they will quite likely precipitate a realignment of the political cultures. Existing coalitions (such as that between the individualists and the hierarchists that gave us the energy orthodoxy of the 1970s) are undermined by the surprises, and new coalitions (such as those that are now linking the libertarian and Green critiques of orthodoxy) begin to form. Our knowledge of the natural constraints, therefore, comes to us in an indirect way. It is they that impart the erratic pattern of alternation to the process of technology that the cultural constraints drive.

But realists will still not be satisfied. There is, they will insist, only one world so how can it be pluralized by ideas – myths of nature – that, having no real existence, cannot even be a part of that one world? We would reply, following Alfred North Whitehead (1926:228), that these myths are *eternal objects*. An eternal object is not directly accessible; it is not something that just sits there waiting to be examined. Its metaphysical status, rather, is located at one remove from phenomena (which, of course, is why the myths do not get inextricably caught up in history, in actualities). The essence of an eternal object lies not in the actuality itself – the actual happening – but in the possibility for that actuality. Eternal objects (like ways of worldmaking) have to do not with phenomena but with the possibility of phenomena, and these two levels are brought into relationship with one another by a third factor: the eternal objects' mode of ingression into the actuality. This mode of ingression *is* accessible. It reveals itself to us in the form of recurrent identifiable elements (commitments, justifications, triumphs, tragedies, strategies, surprises, and so on) in our interactions with everything that is not us: our fellow humans and our circumambient cosmos. The deep reality that cultural theory enables us to get to grips with is our diverse involvements in the one world we all inhabit.

Now, with these philosophical loose ends tidied away, we can get on with the practical implications of all this: how best to handle risks and uncertainties, how to assess technology, and how to institute the exploratory mode.

Notes

1. 'We' here refers to Michael Thompson, Richard Caputo and Karen Closek.

2. Although the deep gas hypothesis of Tom Gold, Ed Schmidt and others now disputes even this last shred of certainty.

3. This section on oil and gas reserves estimation draws upon the findings of a research project with which one of us was associated (Wildavsky and Tenenbaum 1981).

4. How else could one account for the existence, within the US Department of Energy, of an Office of Data Validation whose task it is to tell the department which of its own data it can believe?

5. How near or far the 'business as usual' future is makes no difference to the course that has to be steered to reach it. This means that the last logical possibility – the answer: yes, yes – is redundant.

6. The very word 'decouple' betrays the bureaucratic paradigm: 'de – prefix much used in Civil Service jargon in coining words expressing undoing or ridding' (Chambers Twentieth Century Dictionary).

Chapter 7

Dissolving Risks into Technologies and Technologies into Ways of Life

Risk assessment and technology assessment have, in recent years, been the great growth areas in science for public policy. They have burgeoned with acronymous methodologies, such as QRA (quantitative risk assessment; in the United States it is known as PRA, probabilistic risk assessment), RBA (risk–benefit analysis) and CTA (constructive technology assessment), they have developed their own specialized communities with their own conferences and journals, and they have in many countries crystallized out into impressive formal institutions, of which the US Office of Technology Assessment (OTA) is perhaps the most striking example. 'Ivory tower academics' and 'hard-nosed policy types' have been able to come together around a single, simple aim: to find out what the consequences of various technologies really are; to discover just what risks they do and do not bring with them. It is this mutuality of perceived interests that has provided the impetus for the spectacular growth of risk assessment and technology assessment.

However, the very process of pursuing this common aim has revealed just how unattainable it is. Many of the consequences of technology, it turns out, are not just unanticipated; they are unanticipable:

A distinctive characteristic of our natural world is that it typically is not and cannot be known to the desired degree of precision. (Slovic *et al.* 1979:370)

At the same time, this focus on the *unanticipated consequences* of technologies has directed attention away from their *inconsequent anticipations*; those consequences that are clearly discerned before-hand yet never, in fact, materialize. This is an unfortunate omission, since the real test of an assessment is not the number of consequences that are anticipated, but that number less those that turn out to have been inconsequent anticipations. Let us give a little historical example to drive home this crucial, and currently disregarded, point.

The Ganges Canal, which when it was opened in 1854, eliminated the recurrent famines that for centuries had plagued the vast area between the Jumna and Ganges Rivers, applied technological solutions that had been perfected by the Mughals more than a century earlier. Yet, for all this project's lack of novelty, the technology assessments of the day were seriously wide of the mark, scoring three inconsequent anticipations to just one anticipated consequence:

> It was said that earthquakes would destroy the viaducts, that miasmas would hang over the irrigated lands, that malaria would become rife and that the navigation of the Ganges would be affected. (This last objection was the only one that proved to be right.) (Newby 1966:61)

Of course, it will be argued that technology assessment has improved beyond all comparison since those amateurish days, but even so, there will always be more than a whiff of hubris in the claim that everything has been anticipated. And this, ultimately, is the claim that technology assessment has to make.[1] It has to make this claim because it has set out by assuming that anticipation is the way to go: the *only* way to go.

Given this heroic assumption, an unanticipated consequence, or an unassessed risk, is always a failure: something that should have been spotted but was not. But the trouble is that this pervasive gloom is not something that is in any way inherent in the unanticipated; it is, rather, a quality that is imposed upon the unanticipated by those whose satisfaction in life comes only from anticipation. The whole assessment business, in other words, is culturally biased. Since our cultural theory is concerned with identifying biases and then understanding their institutional origins, we have to treat the assessment approach, not as *the* way to study and handle our interactions with our physical world, but as just *one* of the culturally plural modes that, through their contentions, shape our involvement with it. So we begin by asking whether there are not other, less negative, ways of coping with the unanticipable.

It is an ill wind, so the optimistic saying goes, that blows nobody any good. Much the same is often true of unanticipated consequences; sometimes (like the vacuum cleaner[2]) they even blow (or should we say suck?) everyone some good. And, in much the same way, risk is often opportunity: something to be actively courted not negatively avoided (Wildavsky 1988). Those adventurous and opportunistic individuals who go around grasping nettles tightly and reaping the benefits of any happy accidents that come their way are inevitably something of an affront to those who have chosen the anticipatory mode. But, as E.M. Forster has pointed out, the real tragedy of our time is not the man who is taken unprepared but the man who has prepared and is never taken. 'On a tragedy of that kind', Forster continues, warming to his critique of the anticipatory mode, 'our morality is duly silent. It assumes that preparation against danger is in itself a good, and that men, like nations, are the better for staggering through life fully armed' (from *Howard's End*).

Staggering through life fully armed, we could say, is the pathology of the anticipatory mode. As we anticipate more and more of the things that may happen to us so we encumber ourselves with more and more specialized devices, each designed to cope with just one hitherto unanticipated consequence. Outward Bound students on modest summer rambles have found themselves benighted because of the rucksacks full of emergency rations, sleeping bags, tents, torches, flares and space blankets that they are required to carry in order to cope with all the specific situations that have been antici- pated by those who have been charged with responsibility for their safety. But when we look at those who have made themselves at home in the hills (shepherds and mountaineers) we find that they do not do this. They travel light (but not foolhardily), relying on generalized resources such as knowledge, skill and experience, rather than specialized devices, to cope with the unexpected. They learn how to pace themselves, when to turn back, how to read changes in the weather conditions, when to push on and when to sit tight. These things they learn by reflecting on their own experiences, by exchanging experiences with others, by deliberately courting danger ('winding their necks out' as mountaineers say) and by treating all the unanticipated events that befall them as a valuable store of raw material from which to extract more of the generalized resources upon which they rely.

As we go from specialized devices ('staggering through life fully armed') to generalized resources ('travelling light') so we go from the anticipatory mode to the serendipitatory mode. Some writers (Wildavsky 1988), critical of the risk-averse assumptions that are built into contemporary risk assessment and technology assessment, have spoken of this currently neglected mode as *resilience*, but we prefer (following Holling (1979, 1986), the pioneer of this notion) to reserve 'resilience', not for the mode itself, but for the particular blend of anticipation and serendipity (and, as we will show presently, of a third mode, taboo or *sacrosanctification*) that enables a culturally plural *regime* to ride with, and make the most of, all the changes that it both experiences and contributes to. How, we ask, can the pluralized whole arrange itself in such a way as to ensure that some of its parts effectively anticipate the anticipatable whilst others of its parts successfully interrogate the unknown, and still others of its parts tell us which stones are best left unturned? That, we believe, is the question to ask if we wish to intervene constructively in the largely unconscious processes by which resilience is, and always has been, secured.

To ask this question, and to shift the whole emphasis away from anticipation *per se* and onto the possibility of improving the constructive interplay of culturally plural modes, is to suggest that both technology and risk are not at all what they are commonly assumed to be. So, before we can get on to thinking about regimes as institutionally plural arrangements for promoting the constructive interplay of these different modes, we will need to rethink our ideas about technology and risk.

What is Technology? What is Risk?

Technologies are not like job applicants. They do not present themselves to us as fully formed and discrete entities. Rather, we and they are all bound up together. Though we may speak of 'new technologies' there are really only new technological developments. A 'new technology' is always a retrospective label that we attach to certain sections in the whole flow of technological developments that seem to us to be markedly different from what has preceded them and from what surrounds them. By the time we recognize a technology as new we are already committed to it. We simply cannot catch, and select, our technologies before we become committed to them; that option is available to us only in relation to the little pieces – the new developments – that, in retrospect, we can see were the crucial ingredients of the new technology. We can, of course, choose to get rid of a new technology; what we cannot do is choose not to have it in the first place.[3]

This seemingly awkward predicament is the source of Collingridge's celebrated 'control dilemma': at the time we can do something about a new technology we don't know enough about it and, by the time we do know enough about it, it's too late (Collingridge 1980). Cultural theory takes a less anguished view, dissolving away the control dilemma by exposing the fallacy embedded in the very idea that technology can be, and should be, brought under some kind of 'external' social control.

Cultural theory tells us that technology is a social process and that that process is driven by the contention of the various assessments that each cultural bias makes of each new technological development. Once we see that social control (albeit in this pluralized and contentious form) is what actually makes technology possible, then 'the social control of technology' – the concept that gives us the control dilemma – becomes 'the social control of social control'. Of course there *is* a serious message in Collingridge's control dilemma, but it is not the message that technology needs to be brought under social control. Rather, the message is that the social controls that make technology possible do not automatically interact in such a way as to produce the best available outcome. Indeed, as Collingridge shows so clearly, they often interact in such a way as to entrench us in a particular sequence of technological developments that actually prevents us from gaining access to other outcomes that would have been available to us had we not got ourselves entrenched. Avoiding that sort of situation (minimizing physical and social inflexibility) is what the securing of resilience is all about, and to do that we need to understand what the assessment process that we wish to intervene constructively in is.

This view of technology, in which risk assessments and social controls are the necessary conditions for its existence, is so far removed from the assumption that has been built into risk assessment and technology assessment – that technology is something outside of social life that then has impacts on it – that there is little point in our playing around with present approaches in the hope of modifying them to cope with the idea that we and our technologies are all caught up together in a complex process of development that, here and there, may offer some chance for constructive intervention.[4] Much better to start again from scratch.

1.   Views of the world, visions of the future, convictions as to what

is possible and impossible, natural and unnatural, rational and irrational, and many, many other determinants of our behaviour are intimately connected to different preferred patterns of social relationships, all of which are inescapable features of complex industrial societies.[5]

2. The holders of such views and visions tend to act in ways that, so far as they can judge, will tend to strengthen their preferred way of life and to weaken those of others.

3. This is the structured and heterogeneous environment into which all technological developments are born, and it promotes all sorts of pressures for and against their adoption (and, indeed for and against their birth and even their conception).

4. Such developments, even if adopted, first have to find their way through all the obstacles that those who are opposed to them erect and, second, to mesh constructively with what already exists *or* to modify what already exists until it meshes constructively with them.

5. And, of course, all this selection for social acceptability has to be physically possible. Nature does have some vetoes, even though we can never know what they all are.

Technology, in other words, is a turbulent social process and its evolution is probably more complex than we can ever know. But we *can* set out the conditions for technology to be possible (that is what the above list does) and we *can* explore parts of this process with which we are familiar, with these conditions in mind, so as to get a 'feel' for the sorts of things that must be going on and, more importantly, for the sorts of things that could not be going on. Good design, we argue, should comport with the former and distance itself from the latter. For instance, the lavatory rim-block made the transition from bad design to good design once the designers became sensitized to the Greens' engineering aesthetic as well as those of the hierarchists and the individualists.

So our idea of constructive intervention is modest and exploratory: a self-reflexive and sympathetic input to the design process, rather than a lofty hubristic judgement on entire technologies. It is, in many ways, the opposite of risk assessment and technology assessment. This input to the design process can be summarized in the following way.

Our cultural theory provides us with a usefully short repertoire (or checklist) of socially viable biases for the selection of risks and of the technologies that those risks stand as proxies for. Then, when we look at any particular lines of technological developments, we can 'deconstruct' what has been happening (physically and socially) in terms of these viable biases, each of which, so the theory runs, has its essential contribution to make. If some biases are completely excluded, or if those that are present are interacting in ways that we know (from our accumulated and accumulating understanding of these sorts of interactions in other areas) give rise to serious inflexibilities and widespread social concern, then the little red warning lights should start blinking.

QRA versus CRA

One of the great disappointments for those who have pinned their hopes on quantitative risk assessment (QRA; PRA in the United States), on finding out what the risks associated with a technology really are, is that even when they manage to do this, people don't believe them. When their 'misperceptions' are pointed out to them, people seldom do the 'rational' thing and realign their perceptions with those of the expert. Are we to conclude, therefore, that people are irrational? More practically, whether they are rational or not, how (if we are policy makers) do we cope with a situation which resolutely refuses to sort itself out in the way we were led to believe it would? Should policies be based on what the risks really are, or should they be based on what people persist in believing them to be?

Cultural theory's response to these dilemmas is akin to that of the Dubliner unable to give directions to the American visitor to his native city: 'ah, but Oi wouldn't have started from here'. Cultural theory, rather, starts by insisting that, though they may do daft things from time to time, people by and large are not daft. They are, in other words, rational, and if they do different things and espouse different certainties then the sources of these systematic variations are to be found in the different contexts in which they are living and acting. Risk assessment, it tells us, is like cat-skinning: there is more than one way of doing it. Quantitative risk assessment, we know, is *one* way of doing it; casual risk assessment enables us to get at the other ways of doing it:

Each of us, every day, takes calculated risks. But how do we do the calculation? Not through whatever grasp we may have of statistics or probability theory, that's for certain. Ultimately it's a matter of

temperament, but we bring this casual risk assessment into our public
activities as well as our personal lives.

This is why Windscale, the prospect of Sizewell B, as well as the
results of risk-taking at Chernobyl, set us all wondering about those
who calculate risks on our behalf (Ward 1987:29, in a review of Douglas
1985 and Thompson *et al.* 1986).

Casual risk assessment, we can now see, is much less simple than
quantitative risk assessment. Wrapped up in the assessment of the
risk itself there is also a judgement on the trustworthiness of the
institution that is responsible for that risk, and an expression of just
how agreeable or disagreeable is the technology that sustains that
institution and generates that risk.

But in quantitative risk assessment the institution, without which
neither the risk itself nor the technology that generates it could exist,
does not enter into the calculation. Or, at least, if we do what cultural
theory tells us to do and treat QRA *as* CRA we can say that the
trustworthiness of the institution is always assessed at 100 per cent.
So QRA, as we might expect since it is only one way of doing it, is
really just a special case of CRA: one in which the credibility of the
supporting institution is not to be doubted. And the other ways,
we may expect, will separate out as we look into the sorts of social
and physical contexts that are not so conducive to the maintenance
of institutional trust and technological entrenchment.

So, if it is the cultural biases that select our risks and our
technologies for us, we will need to understand the different
preferred ways of life that go with each of those cultural biases. We
will also have to accept that, contrary to the assumptions that have
been built into technological decision making there is nothing
special about risks and technologies; like everything else in this
world, risks and technologies are selected so as to rationalize, justify
and promote preferred ways of life. Our cultural argument, in
rejecting the prevalent idea that technology is some autonomous
force outside of social processes, seriously undermines the claims
that have been made for risk assessment and for technology assessment. These esoteric techniques, it tells us, are not objective
evaluations of what our engineers are doing; they are beautifully
crafted elaborations of just one of the cultural biases that together
make engineering, and hence technology, possible. They do not
stand outside engineering; they are one part of it.

It is precisely because there is no cosmic exile, no way of standing
outside of our technology, that we insist that the only sort of

conscious intervention that stands any chance of being constructive will be one that is integral to the design process. Since the argumentation that has brought us to this point is sociological (in the widest sense of the word), and since the design process is not usually seen as belonging to the social sciences, we will now have to effect a rather unlikely synthesis: anthropology and engineering. And risk – the pluralized nature of its perception – is the key to this synthesis.

Engineering and Anthropology: Is There a Difference?

Risk assessment, 'the new science of risk assessment' (Silcock 1979), as it has been hailed, sets out to do three things: to *quantify* the dangers of modern technology, to *compare* them, and to *devise* rational policies for dealing with them. Though the techniques of risk assessment are mathematical and at times complex, its con-clusions are simple enough and are often displayed in the form of risk tables for a variety of activities: coalmining, rock climbing, hang-gliding, and so on, each with its appropriate odds, such as 'the chances of being killed rock climbing are one in 13,000 in any one year'. Once the risks have been quantified and compared in this way, it is but a short step to marry risk assessment to cost–benefit analysis (and a particular sort of engineering to a particular sort of economics) to produce RBA (risk–benefit analysis), the technique that, among other things, places an exact money value on a human life: US$287,175 (Hapgood 1979). Two stages are involved; first, determining the risks of various accidents within each technology or activity and, second, making the comparisons and drawing the policy conclusions from them. The argument in favour of risk assessment runs something like this:

> *Method*: The simplest way to put the risks of big technology into perspective is to compare them with the risks we run in everyday life.

> *Application*: In any gamble it is foolish not to find the odds since these are the only rational means we have of taking vital decisions, not only about personal safety but also about national policy (Silcock 1979).

Our little excursion into casual risk assessment tells us that, before accepting these seemingly reasonable and innocuous claims, we should ask the following questions:

1. Can risk assessment tell us what the risks in a big technology, such as nuclear power, really are?
2. Is the comparison with other risks valid and meaningful?
3. If we cannot find out what the odds are does it follow that we cannot act rationally?
4. If the answer to question 3 is 'no', what are these other rational modes of decision taking?
5. If the real odds (assuming they can be determined) are not matched by individuals' perceptions of the odds should they override *individual values* in arriving at the best *social choice*?
6. Since risk assessment has only existed for ten years or so, we know that social choices can be arrived at without this ruthless, direct comparison of risks, but we do not know whether the reverse is true. That is, we do not know whether social choice is possible *with* total comparability. To put the question at its starkest: are risk assessment and democracy inimical?

Then we should query some of the basic, but implicit, assumptions in risk assessment.

7. That all risk is nasty.
8. That it is always more desirable to know the odds than not to know the odds.
9. That there is a difference in kind (i.e., a non-comparability) between just two categories of risk: *voluntary* and *involuntary*.

Finally, we should ask this question:

10. If risk assessment is only one out of several rational modes of decision taking why should it be that some individuals and institutions should be so attracted to it as to believe, not only that it is the best, but that it is the only mode?

Of course, as anyone familiar with the risk debate will point out, each of these ten questions has been asked, and answered, by someone, somewhere. Taken together they provide, not a new point of departure, but a convenient means of summarizing all the serious criticisms that, over the years, have been levelled at risk assessment. But they do much more than simply list the shortcomings of risk assessment; they turn the scientific tables on it. Although these criticisms have been seen by the self-professed 'hard scientists' as the negative and unhelpful carpings of a bunch of radically motivated softies, the fact is that these carpings, put together, are the scientific approach to risk.

So these ten questions are a *research programme*: a strategy for establishing a coherent, usable and scientific framework for guiding decision making on technology. Since each of these questions has already been asked and answered, the task we face is not so much one of creation as of assembly. Even so, it is a considerable undertaking and not one that can be achieved with any measure of conviction and comprehension in a little book like this. So we will restrict ourselves here to conveying the feel – the essential character – of the scientific approach to risk by exploring the answers to just two of these questions: numbers 1 and 3.

Question 1: Can risk assessment tell us what the risks in a big technology really are?

Leaving aside the philosophical objections that can be raised over the odds that a penny will come down heads when you have called tails (Keynes 1973), we should look carefully at what is involved in the extension of probabilistic reasoning from coin tossing to high technology. As you go from the flip of a penny to the meltdown of a reactor core so you go from a closed system to an open system: from science to engineering. The engineer, of course, does use a lot of science but, unlike the experimental scientist, he does not work on the laboratory bench, he works in the world. His skill, his judgement and his art lie not so much in his mastery of the science he is using as in his handling of the inescapable tension between the closed system assumptions of that science (the ideal gas, the black body, the coin that cannot land on its edge) and the open system reality (the possibility of unconsidered and unconsiderable outcomes) of the world in which he is working. That is what engineering *is*. That, as engineers well know, is the source of their dignity: the unique foundation on which their entire profession is built (Chilver 1975, Muir Wood 1980).

This is an absurdly simple and elementary distinction – first-year (first-day, even) engineering course stuff. Nor is it a distinction drawn from the outside, by social scientists or philosophers. It is an engineering distinction; it is the engineer's own understanding of what he is. All we are going to do (from the outside, as it were) is take this distinction and see how risk assessment measures up to it. Even then, we will rely heavily on those on the inside – engineers – to guide us.

Octavius Critchley (an engineer and a member of the Nuclear Installations Inspectorate of the British Health and Safety Executive) has developed this closed system/open system argument clearly and forcibly and has asked why the inappropriate quantitative methodology of the bench scientist should increasingly be applied to nuclear installations, especially when the appropriate qualitative methodology of the engineer that was employed until recently has been so successful that 'no one has been killed nor has anyone been injured by radiation on any nuclear site'. He goes on to provide the answer:

> The Rasmussen (1975) Safety Study [which was based on *quantitative* safety analysis] assesses the accident risks for a large atomic power programme at orders less than that to which people in the USA are exposed in normal living. Though it specifically avoids making any recommendations, a decision maker would conclude on scientific grounds that nuclear power is an acceptable risk . . . interest in this kind of prophecy has increased greatly and diverse methods of prediction and especially systems analysis have flourished under the stimulus and encouragement of politicians and administrators. The apparent reduction of dilemmas to a choice between numerical values is attractive because it enables proximate decision makers to compensate for lack of knowledge of the disciplines involved and this is especially so in technology (Critchley 1978).

If Critchley is right, then we have here an example of the replacement of an appropriate methodology by an inappropriate one as a result of political and organizational pressures. Could it be that we are getting, not the best available management of technological risk, but the most administratively convenient one? To ask this question is to open up an altogether different approach to risk, an approach that focuses not so much on the risks themselves as on what they are being used *for*.

What kind of a social being, we should now ask ourselves, sets a high value on administrative convenience? And what kind of a world would furnish him with a repertoire of risks conveniently arranged for him to administer? The answer to the first question is: someone in the upper reaches of a large hierarchical organization. And the answer to the second question is: a world that is both finite and fixable. We can then go on and say that such a social being is behaving rationally if he insists (often largely at the behest of his unquestioned assumptions – his *a priori*) that that is how the world is.

Now, by introducing the notion of worldmaking – of socially malleable ideas of nature (Thompson 1988) – we have uncovered a plausible rationale for the risk assessor's seemingly irrational urge to attempt the impossible. And we also have a plausible explanation both for his resistance to the 'uncertainty principle' inherent in the open system view of risk and for the technocratic tenacity with which he clings to his closed system/bench science account of it all. Completeness, closure, clarity, compartmentalization and control: These are the great claims that stabilize and justify hierarchical organization. If a hierarchical organization aspires to handle technological risk then it will be predisposed (for the soundest of organizational reasons) towards accepting and insisting on three things: first, a closed system view of the world within which all risks are discoverable and measurable, second, a fixable nature within which those with the requisite skill and expertise can exercise control and, third, a definition of scientific rationality that emphasizes specialization, predictability, quantification and certainty creation.

But this, of course, is only one socially induced rationality and we should now press on to enquire what others can, and do, exist and what kinds of social organization they variously help to stabilize. The idea of this approach is to tease out the various plural rationalities (Grauer *et al.* 1985), not with a view to determining which one is right (that is a meaningless question) but, rather, with the view that each will be appropriate in certain, specifiable circumstances and inappropriate in others. And as we move from rightness to appropriateness – from the adversary mode to the exploratory mode – so the variety and contradiction of management modes ceases to be an obstacle to the implementation of rational policies and becomes a valuable resource; perhaps the ultimate resource. But to harness this resource we first have to overcome the narrow tyranny of the particular rationality that, as Critchley rightly fears, is currently driving out other, often more appropriate, rationalities from the whole field of technology assessment and risk management. To do this we must query that orientation's central assumption: that quantification is a precondition for scientific rationality.

Question 3: If we cannot find out what the odds are does it follow that we cannot act rationally?

Risks can entail four sorts of uncertainty. First, when we toss a coin we are uncertain whether it will come down heads but (certain philosophical provisos apart) at least we know what the odds are that it will do so. Second, we know that a particular accident can occur (in a nuclear power station, say) but we are uncertain as to its likelihood. Third, we may be uncertain as to whether something that we know can happen is dangerous or not. Fourth, we may not even be aware of the existence of that something that may or may not be dangerous.

Within economics the first two correspond to the celebrated distinction between 'risk' and 'uncertainty' (Knight 1921), whilst the last two are either ignored or uncritically subsumed under 'uncertainty' (Elster 1979). Engineering is rather more discerning. There, the first kind of uncertainty is handled by experiment. In an experiment there is a complete theory predicting the behaviour of the system and the system itself can be isolated (put on the experimenter's bench, as it were), subjected to certain carefully controlled changes, and its behaviour observed to see whether it is consistent with the predictions of the theory. The second kind of uncertainty is handled by test. In this case there is no complete theory but the system itself can be isolated and put through a realistic series of changes to see what happens to it. The third kind of uncertainty (where even testing is not feasible) is handled, first, by conceding that it exists and, second, by drawing upon a wealth of shared experience in the handling of that sort of thing. The notions of the maximum credible accident (MCA) and the maximum hypothetical accident (MHA) and the way they are then related to the design criteria within the site and to the selection criteria for the site itself, respectively, provide an example of how this sort of uncertainty has been handled. The last kind of uncertainty calls for the full exercise of the engineer's open-systems art. 'Cockcroft's Folly', the vents on the top of the Windscale piles that averted a major accident of a type that, at the time of construction, was not conceivable, is an example of this sort of 'sound engineering judgement'.

Bench science, by contrast, restricts itself to the experiment, and this can lead to some interesting confusions. The Rasmussen reactor safety study, for instance, adopts this bench science approach for the construction of its vast fault tree within which each box (each possible fault) is given a numerical probability. Once you have such a tree you can derive, by impeccable logic, the probabilities of particular accidents that can result from particular concatenations of faults. All you have to do is multiply the probabilities in the boxes along the particular sequences of faults that can lead to those particular accidents. But the engineer is reluctant to do this, preferring instead the woolliness of his 'sound engineering judgement' to the exercise of a clear-cut and indisputable logic. Now the incomprehension, and exasperation, start.[6]

'Do you disagree with the probabilities?', the risk assessor asks.

'No', replies the engineer. 'Do you disagree with the fault tree, with the chains of events that can lead to certain accidents?', the risk assessor asks. 'No', replies the engineer. 'Then how can you possibly object to the multiplying of the probabilities?', demands the risk assessor. 'Oh, I don't object to all such multiplications', says the engineer, 'just this one here, and this one, and that one there', pointing to particular branches within the fault tree. This is too much for the risk assessor. To him, a tree is a tree is a tree. 'How', he cries, 'can you possibly justify accepting multiplication along some branches and not along others?'.

'Ah, it's perfectly simple', says the engineer. 'See that box there, labelled "can-splitting"? Its probability was arrived at by experiment. That box there, labelled "can-popping", its probability was arrived at by a series of tests. And that box there, something to do with a possible pipe system failure, its probability was arrived at by getting a number of leading experts together, giving them a good lunch, and then asking them for their best estimates and taking the average. I would accept the multiplication of probabilities arrived at by experiment. I would accept the individual probabilities arrived at by test, but not their multiplication, and I would neither multiply nor accept probabilities of the third kind, preferring instead to use these numbers as just a rough (but still valuable) qualitative guide. And then, of course, I would note that the fault tree does not allow for Irish labourers urinating into the housings for the post-stressed reinforcing cables of the containment vessel whilst the plant was under construction, and I would like to be able to take that sort of thing into account as well.'[7]

So where does all this leave the risk assessor (not to mention his inexpert client, the decision maker)? His prior commitment to a closed-system/bench-science approach leaves only one strategic avenue open to him. His sole aim has to be to convert all this uncertainty to the coin-tossing kind – to determine what the risks for each box really are – and his justification for this inescapable strategic commitment is the assertion that if we do not know what the odds are we do not have any 'rational means of taking vital decisions, not only about personal safety, but also about national policy'. Such certainty creation would, of course, be fine as a strategy if everything could be made certain. Alas, if there is one thing of which we *can* be certain it is that we cannot be certain of everything.

So what are we to do about all that uncertainty that remains, even after the risk assessor has calculated every risk he can calculate? Well, for a start, we can ask whether it is indeed true that people cannot act rationally in the face of incalculable risks. The answer (hardly surprisingly, since probability was only invented a few centuries ago (Hacking 1975), whilst people have been taking risky decisions for millennia) is no. People can, and do, act rationally when confronted by such risks. What is more (and this is where the political culture of risk comes into the picture) their rational actions sometimes deliberately impose incalculability upon risks that are perfectly calculable. That is, they deliberately and rationally follow a course of action that runs exactly counter to the one which the risk assessor has to insist is the only rational one!

Myopic opportunism and its far-sighted rival: Two risk-handling rationalities and their interaction

'I say, I say, I say', cries the omniscient and unstoppable music hall comedian. 'I don't wish to know that', protests his ineffectual stooge. As with art, so with life. To many happy-go-lucky individuals there is something inherently distasteful about the risk assessor's relentless pursuit of the risks of everything and, sensing this, they begin setting up the barricades, laying the false trails and putting down the smokescreens:

> People who claim to know jackrabbits will tell you that they are primarily motivated by fear, stupidity and craziness. But I have spent enough time in jackrabbit country to know that most of them lead pretty dull lives; they are bored with their daily routines: eat, fuck, sleep, hop around a bush now & [sic] then ... no wonder some of them drift over the line into cheap thrills once in a while; there has to be a powerful adrenalin rush in crouching by the side of the road, waiting for the next set of headlights to come along, then streaking out of the bushes with split-second timing and making it across to the other side just inches in front of the speeding wheels (Thompson 1980:206).

Hunter Thompson is sending up the straights by outrageously acting the part of the anthropologist who, having done his fieldwork among the jackrabbits, actually understands the rationale behind their seemingly irrational behaviour.

And he is right. His little bit of fun-poking reveals two impressively contradictory rationalities: that of the jackrabbits (as interpreted by the anthropologist who has lived among them) and that of the people who 'claim to know jackrabbits'. But there is an interesting asymmetry in their descriptions. The anthropologist is concerned simply to establish the legitimacy of the jackrabbits' rationality,[8] whilst those who claim to know jackrabbits are concerned to impose their own rationality on others, and this they do, not just by pointing out the legitimacy of what they themselves do, but by going one step further and denying the legitimacy of what others (jackrabbits, among them) do. The first is prepared to countenance a plurality of rationalities; the second is not. The first is tolerant of contradiction; the second is not, and it sustains itself (and advances its imperialist aims) by making accusations of irrationality against the others.

The study of witchcraft got nowhere until anthropologists stopped looking at witchcraft itself and looked instead at witchcraft accusations (Evans-Pritchard 1937). Much the same, we suggest, holds for irrationality. Whilst psychologists and philosophers argue endlessly over whether or not human irrationality can ever be demonstrated,[9] the irrationality accusations and their revealing patterns – Lord Rothschild's (1978) intemperate remarks about 'eco-freaks and eco-nuts', for instance, and the no less intemperate responses of the Greens – are being laid out for any who have eyes to see them. Just map the small number of directions in which the various accusing fingers are pointed and the offending rationalities (and their institutional origins) are soon revealed in all their antagonistic splendour.

Himalayan mountaineers, for instance (both Europeans and Sherpas), follow the jackrabbit strategy of rejecting readily available information about the long term so as to be able to concentrate opportunistically on just those few (but large) risks that swim into their short-term ken (Thompson 1980). When this strategy is related to the sorts of individualized contexts in which they operate, the behaviour of these mountaineers makes a good deal of sense. We may not approve of what they are doing, of course, but there *is* a rationale behind it, a rationale that is based on the shrewd and daring assessment of the risks they face in the here-and-now, not in terms of the readily available historical data for the activity they are engaged in, but in terms of their own skill, experience and judgement. In other words, they go to considerable institutionalized lengths (these strategies being rooted in enduring patterns of social relations, rather than in the individuals' personalities) not to know the odds they face.

Set against this, the risk assessor's insistence that rational decisions are possible only when you know the odds begins to look more like an irrationality accusation than a value-free statement of fact. One of the best ways of stopping people from doing something you do not want them to do is, first, to state authoritatively that it is impossible to do it and, second, to label as deviant (irrational) those who nevertheless attempt to do it. Is this what the risk assessors and the hazard managers, unwittingly and from the best of intentions, are doing to the rest of us? (Clark 1980).[10]

At this point in the argument the exasperated risk assessor will usually enquire whether we seriously expect anyone to believe that the best way to manage the risks in high technology is to close our eyes to them. Of course, we do not. All we are saying is that his strategy of certainty creation is only *one* of the socially available ways of handling risk. From this it follows that we should be doing everything that we can to transcend the narrow provincialism that closes in the moment we demand to know which is the *right* way, and that we should begin, coolly and dispassionately, by discovering what these different risk handling styles are. That is where the cultural theory would have us start from.

Since each style has been around for generations, and since each contradicts all the others, there must be *something* in it; it must be effective in *certain* circumstances; if it wasn't it wouldn't still be around. Each, therefore, has *something* to contribute. What we need, therefore, are two things: a lexicon of risk-handling styles and a set of selection criteria that will help us to understand (often against our own provincial convictions) just when and where each is most appropriate, and just when and where each is least appropriate. That we submit, is the proper (and achievable) aim of a scientific approach to risk.

Notes

1. The term technology assessment was coined in the late 1960s by Congressman Emilio Dadario of Connecticut who, as chairman of the House Subcommittee on Science, Research and Development, 'became aware of the need for policy-makers in the technologically advanced societies to anticipate the consequences of future technological developments as well as the need for institutional mechanisms to undertake this task' (Segal 1982). Over the last decade or so, institutions such as the US Office of Technology Assessment have become more modest, focusing more on analyses of public policy that are limited to comparing different policy options (Dickson 1984).

2. The vacuum cleaner has virtually removed the human flea, and

the diseases it carries, from the advanced industrialized nations: a consequence that was not anticipated in the early years of that technology's development.

3. Thomas Hughes, historian of technology, speaks of the 'inertia' or 'conservative momentum' of technological systems: the organizations, principles, attitudes and intentions, as well as technical components that are deeply embedded within technological systems (1989).

4. The practitioners of TA, however, have now moved strongly in this direction, and there now exists (especially in the United States, in places like Oak Ridge National Laboratory and Clark University) a 'hands-on state of the art' that increasingly concerns itself with the cultural pluralism and the 'constructive ambiguity' to which that pluralism gives rise. The trouble, however, is that these practitioners have had to introduce these modifications in the face of the assumptions (especially that anticipation is *the* way to go) upon which Congressman Dadario founded TA. The practitioners, in their hands-on wisdom, have moved strongly in the right direction but the theory has not been able to follow them. Our aim is to give them the theory they need (and to do what we can to rubbish the theory they need to be rid of).

5. They are also essential ingredients of *any* society, the only difference being that all four biases may not always be discernible in pre-industrial societies.

6. We say 'the risk assessor' and 'the engineer' because the account that follows is of an exchange between a risk assessor and an engineer that we were fortunate enough to witness. Whilst this exchange exactly captured the distinction we are drawing here, we would not wish to suggest that all engineers measure up to this particular paragon or that all risk assessors are as closed-in as this one. It is their founding assumptions that concern us here.

7. Most of the labourers on these construction sites are Irish. At tea and meal breaks they consume considerable quantities of tea (and sometimes beer) and are reluctant, when nature has taken its course, to make the laborious and time-wasting descent from their lofty scaffold. Since their Hibernian modesty precludes the alternative adopted by some of their younger (and more exhibitionist) English colleagues, they make discreet use of the concrete openings so conveniently positioned along their work station. Such is the structure of authority and control on the site that the information concerning the ultimate purpose of these openings – information that, if they possessed it, might close this option to them – cannot reach them.

8. Anthropology has been well defined by Clifford Geertz (1973) as the deprovincialization of rationality.

9. The experimental work of two psychologists, Daniel Kahneman and

Amos Tversky (1982), suggests that people do not behave according to the postulates of economic rationality and that, moreover, they are incapable of doing so. Some (Nisbett and Borgida 1975, Slovic *et al.* 1976) have argued that these results have bleak implications for human rationality, only to be confronted by Jonathan Cohen (1981) who holds that 'nothing in the existing literature or in any possible future results of human experimental enquiry could have bleak implications for human rationality'.

Cohen sees the failures in probabilistic reasoning that Kahneman and Tversky have exposed, not as demonstrating a human inability to act rationally, but rather as revealing nothing more than, at best, patterns of illusion and, at worst, the intelligence and education of the subjects. Cohen's position so reverses that of the bleak implicators as to allow us to suggest that he is trying to do for rationality what Gödel did for arithmetic:

> ordinary human reasoning – by which I mean the reasoning of adults who have not been systematically educated in any branch of logic or probability theory – cannot be held to be faultily programmed: it sets its own standards (Cohen 1981).

Just as the non-contradiction of arithmetic can never be proved, Cohen argues, so the irrationality of human behaviour can never be established.

The trouble with this argument, however, is that, in fastening on the individual's *cognitive competence* (his innate ability to reason validly) and his *cognitive performance* (that ability acted upon), it totally ignores his social context (the pattern of his relationships with others) which, cultural theory shows us, is what actually determines whether and by whom an individual's actions will be judged rational or irrational. To speak of the rationality of an act, whilst excluding that which confers rationality upon it, is to speak of nothing at all.

10. The most pronounced critique (empirically and theoretically) of the conventional single-rationality approach to risk management and the regulation of hazardous technologies can be found in the work of Wynne (1987, 1989). His arguments very much concur with ours in that he stresses that risk perceptions and the assessment of 'facts' are grounded in social interaction and social practices.

Chapter 8

Engineering as Tacit Anthropology: The Rules of Closure and the Dynamics of Consent

So we are arguing for an anthropology of risk, which is hardly surprising, since one of us is an anthropologist. What may be surprising, though, is our idea about where we should look for such an anthropology. We could, of course, look at the burgeoning literatures on the cultural theory of risk, on the sociology of science, on the social construction of reality and so on, and this, indeed, is precisely what we have been doing in getting ourselves (and, we hope, our fellow social scientists) to the position we have now reached. However, we do not think this is the best way for social scientists to communicate with engineers, civil servants, policy makers, industrialists, environmentalists and the like; with doers rather than thinkers.

Nor is it only a matter of public relations. In many ways the practitioners (engineers and lawyers, for instance) are way ahead of the social scientists. The fact that all too easily gets overlooked is that, over the centuries, their theories and practices (unlike those of the social scientists) have been hammered out on the anvil of implementation: the criterion of acceptance is not simply that what the professional (using the word in a very broad sense) proposes is consistent and defensible but that it works as well. Or, to be more precise (and this is where the anthropology comes in), the criterion is that what they do is perceived as working well by those who, if they perceived it to be working badly, might react in such a way as to undermine the credibility – the public standing and esteem – of the professional. Professions, to be successful, have to be socially viable; they have to be *mediating* institutions; they have to contain within themselves a variety of approach and definition sufficient to match that which they will encounter among their diverse clients: us. The result is that, although such professions may not be able to provide explicit descriptions of all the various rationalities and risk-handling styles that they continually bump into, they nevertheless do take them into account. They have, as we say in the social sciences, 'internalized' them.

So the role we are advocating for the anthropologist is a modest and, we hope, temporary one. His present task is to get under the skin of the engineer and draw out (we would say 'deconstruct') this internalized understanding. And the reason why he needs to do this now is that the environment of the engineer is now changing so fast that internalization is simply not enough. The engineer, as he passes through the turbulent transition from industrial to so-called post-industrial society, needs a much more explicit understanding of all the artful things he does; he needs a greatly enhanced capacity for self-reflection. The anthropologist's temporary role, therefore, is to provide and polish the looking glass. Or, to put it another way, to give a more explicit and precise account of the nature of engineering judgement so that engineers can more readily resist those forces that are at present acting in such a way as to destroy that judgement.

The turbulent transition

Civil engineering is defined as the harnessing of the great forces in nature for the benefit of mankind. Although electrical and mechanical engineers sometimes chide their civil siblings for not having altered their ways since they put up the pyramids, there is still plenty of mileage left in this ancient definition; all it needs, if it is to see them through the next few millennia, is a shift in emphasis. Historically the benefits have usually been so obvious, and the technical obstacles so challenging, that the engineer's attention has (quite rightly) been focused on just two of the elements that make up this definition: the science that will enable him to understand the great forces and the engineering art that will allow him safely to harness them. All that has now changed. The really knotty problem now is to know what constitutes a benefit. The engineer used not to have to bother himself too much about that question; now he has to; that, in short, is his transitional predicament.

Buckminster Fuller was fond of pointing out that Edison did not need a licence to light up the world. However, the fact is that if Edison wanted to do it now he *would* have to have a licence. Today's genetic engineer is not free to choose his developmental path; those who designed the Abbeystead tunnel[1] were not permitted to push a vent up into the cherished landscape that lay above it (nor did they have the institutional solidarity to refuse to build when this essential exercise of their engineering judgement was curtailed); the snail darter (that 'insignificant fish', as one irate industrialist, the chairman of Shell Transport, called it) halted the construction of dams throughout the United States; the Austrian electorate voted 51 to 49 per cent against the commissioning of their vast (and vastly expensive) nuclear power station at Zwentendorf; the long-suffering residents of Ronan Point in the London borough of Newham finally forced their local authority (and its expert advisers) to reverse its decisions (and the judgements of its advisers) and demolish their expensive but uninhabitable homes.

Those fringe-dwellers, the cranks, the romantics, the eco-freaks and the *lumpenproletariat* who, throughout the long years of the industrial age, could safely be ignored can no longer be ignored. That is the crucial, and perhaps none too palatable, message that the engineer now has to receive and respond to; that is the one great change that the transition to the information society[2] (as it is sometimes called) has wrought in his environment; that is why he has to confront, and update, the internalized understanding that has for so long served him so well.

A shift of emphasis

The essential tension between the precise engineering science of the theorist and the much more judgemental engineering art of the 'hands-on' practitioner has long been internalized by the engineering and design professions. In the particular risk field in which one of us happens to have some practical experience, this tension is nicely captured in the pithy comments of that great mountaineer, Don Whillans.

> There's no two ways about it: the Himalayas are very dangerous. . . .
> People say it's safe if you obey the rules, but they are wrong. If you
> have plenty of experience and understand the place then you have a
> chance of getting out OK but there are so many unexpected, unknown

things that can happen. People call them freak conditions but they happen every few minutes (Whillans 1984).

So here we have the risk assessor (in cultural theory, the hierarchist) going by the book and convinced that he can actually know the unknowable and anticipate the unanticipatable, and the jackrabbit (in cultural theory, the individualist) cheerfully but far from foolhardily accepting the risks that the risk assessor has to insist are not there, and handling the unknowable and the unanticipatable through the exercise of the fine judgement that the continuous experience and understanding of those sorts of things develops.

But there is, of course, a third strategy (in cultural theory, the egalitarian's). Unlike the risk assessor, a person may concede that freak conditions happen every few minutes and, unlike the jackrabbit, he may decide that those risks are simply not acceptable. This strategy (in mountaineering circles it is ascribed to the professional second, the person who holds the rope for the leader but never leads himself) is the one that the engineer used to be able to ignore. This is the risk-handling style that is not as well internalized as it will have to be. Where the engineer used to have to manage the tension between just two positions, he will now have to cope with a three-cornered tug-o'-war. That is the shift of emphasis that he is going to have to make, and the sooner he makes it the less his loss of public esteem will be.

This third position is not easily reconciled with the other two. For all their differences, the risk assessor and the jackrabbit do both accept considerable risks; they differ only in their preferred methods for selecting, accepting and minimizing them (the risk assessor goes in for anticipation; the jackrabbit for serendipity). But this third position declares unacceptable much that the other two find acceptable. It declares vast areas that they see as negotiable to be sacrosanct: 'no-go', or taboo, regions for human activity. We could, therefore, characterize this egalitarian style of risk handling as *sacrosanctification*. As we move from the first two positions towards this third position so many benefits are dramatically transformed into penalties. Inevitably, if the engineer is to take account of this third position he will have to concern himself more and more with the hitherto neglected question: 'what is a benefit?'. In the days before we started to wear holes in the ozone layer (or, at any rate, were unaware that we might be doing such a thing) the debate was only about the particular path along which a technology should be developed; now it is often about whether or not we should develop the technology itself.

The Shifting Dynamics of Consent

As the rim-blocks story shows, this third position now influences not just the debate but the technology itself, steering it away from places to which it would otherwise have gone and towards ones that the other two positions, left to themselves, would never have considered. The dynamics, in other words, have altered.

Look a little closer at these dynamics and we can see that they are the *dynamics of consent*. The egalitarian position did not participate in the actual design of the paradichlorobenzene rim-blocks (that was something that happened inside an organization that could not really make room for egalitarians, and that egalitarians would have selected themselves away from anyway); it simply withdrew its consent when those rim-blocks finally appeared on the market. What is more, it was able to exercise real political muscle: to withdraw its consent in so forceful and public a way as to cause the company to withdraw its product from the market and retreat to the drawing board.[3]

An intelligent organization, once it has experienced such a rebuff, should be able to learn from it. It may not actually bring egalitarians into its design processes (indeed, we doubt whether that would be desirable or possible) but it will at least be able to evaluate those processes from what it now knows to be the egalitarian point of view. In this way it responds, somewhat negatively, to the new cultural and institutional realities of the world in which it is operating. It is then able to develop its technologies in distinctly different directions to those to which it has long been accustomed. But, even so, its heart is still not really in it. This 'heartless commitment', we believe, is the current transitional predicament of most of the large and complex organizations that sustain our production processes (the smaller and simpler organizations tend to learn and adapt, or die, more quickly). The challenge, therefore, is to complete the transition: to help them alter their self-awareness, and their organizational form, so that they can respond positively to the constraints and incentives of the new world they are entering. The challenge is to get them to actually put their hearts into what they are now beginning to do.

We are saying that the world has changed, and that this change is essentially a change in the dynamics of consent. Two large questions, therefore, confront us: why has the world changed, and how has it changed? The first question – the 'why' of the transition – is one that we are not well equipped to answer and that many people, better equipped than we are, are already answering. Though they give many different (and sometimes conflicting) answers, these expert observers are all agreed on one thing: that the world we are entering will be very different from the one we are leaving. We are, they believe, now experiencing changes every bit as dramatic as (but much faster than) those that accompanied the Neolithic and Industrial Revolutions.

Some point to the *harnessing of information* as the characteristic that is rapidly separating us from our familiar technological systems based on the harnessing of energy. Others see a crucial transition from *goods* to *services*: from industrial to post-industrial society. Still others single out the stylistic elision between modernism and post-modernism. Yet others focus on dualisms: dual economies of work-greedy and work-starved populations in the developed world, and stark structural imbalances between the developed world as a whole and the undeveloped world: a Matthew principle ('to those that have shall be given, . . .') operating on both micro- and macro-scales. We live, it would seem, in interesting times; on that there is near-universal agreement. The trouble begins when we try to pin down precisely what it is that makes these times interesting.

Some of these perceptions of what is happening to us all (energy to information and goods to services, for instance) are mutually consistent; simply different but compatible aspects of the same future. But others (the knowledge intensity that is seen as accompanying the 'information society' and structural imbalance, for instance) are mutually contradictory; they are divergent images of divergent and incompatible futures. Since only history will tell us which (if any) of these plausible futures was the right one, all we can do in the here-and-now is burrow down to some of the underlying and shared assumptions from which these various perceptions have diverged. We can, perhaps, narrow these down to the three I's: information, interconnectedness and imbalance.

- Currencies, for instance, can now be traded around the world, and around the clock, in a way that simply was not possible a few years ago. The human organism, which used to be the driving force behind this activity, is now a major drag upon it;

it does not act fast enough. To clear this bottleneck we now rely on computer programs which automatically trigger the buying and selling of currencies in response to various fluctuations in price. Such systems, though they are based on human expertise, are able to act much faster than the experts whose elicited expertise they rely on (nor do they need to eat, sleep or enjoy themselves).[4] Recently we have seen a tidal wave of selling circle the globe before the human experts were able to get around to intervening and moderating the repercussions of what, they clearly realized, was a rather elementary case of the fallacy of composition (what makes sense if only I do it can make nonsense if everyone else does it as well).

- In much the same way, we have recently become aware that the wide scope and dense connectedness of our economic activities can send similar unstoppable pulses through the biosphere that is itself the essential support for all those economic activities. Sawing off the branch you are sitting on used to be just a local surprise; now it can be global. Human activity used to be of little consequence for climate change; now it is the major influence upon it. We know that this is so because of the vast quantities of information (satellite imagery, remote sensing, advances in atmospheric chemistry and in instrumentation, and so on) about the state of the biosphere that are now available to us (Clark and Munn 1986). But the trouble is that the biosphere, like the human organism, often works rather slowly. Nitrates take years to accumulate in groundwater and tens of years to dissipate; rapid changes in carbon dioxide concentrations in the upper atmosphere may even now be triggering the melting of glaciers and ice caps that will not be completed for decades or even centuries; even if we stop their manufacture and use tomorrow, the chlorofluorocarbons already up there in the atmosphere may be sufficient to go on destroying the ozone layer for many years to come. We face the new and alarming possibility that the future has already been planned for us by the aggregated consequences of the myriad deeds we have done. It is, perhaps, this 'new reality' that is now enhancing the legitimacy and standing of the third position – that of the egalitarian – that in the past was quite easily ignored.

These two examples, each of which hinges upon dramatic increases in information, interconnectedness and imbalance, begin to give us some sort of positive hold on what is currently happening to us and to our world. Of course, for all their factual solidity, these three Is are not directly reducible to sustainable and unsustainable avenues of technical change, nor do they offer immediate practical suggestions as to how a nation, a firm, or an individual might best exploit such options. This final step of bringing the three I's down to earth can be effected by asking two seemingly naive questions: 'what is information?' and 'what is technology?'. These, of course, are the questions that cultural theory has us ask. They, we could say, are what give cultural theory its distinctive orientation.

Information, cultural theory tells us, is data organized for decision (organized, in particular, in such a way that the resulting decision can be morally justified). The definition of what is information, therefore, cannot be divorced from he or she who (or that which) does the organizing. This insight emphasizes a crucial difference between information and energy (energy can be defined without reference to the definers) and leads directly to the notion of plural rationality (a notion that, by drawing on all the rows of our chart, can readily be developed into a thoroughgoing organizational theory of information or, if you prefer it, an informational theory of organization; Thompson and Wildavsky 1986a). Technology, too, begins to look quite different from what we habitually see it as. Instead of some exogenous force that advances by its own internal logic and then has impacts *on* society, we begin to realize that technology is a social process: something that simply could not come into existence, and once in existence change and develop, if it were not intimately woven into all the contending institutional strands that, *in toto*, sustain all our social transactions.[5] So it is these strands and their contentions – the cultural biases and the dynamics of consent that they generate – that are the key to understanding technology and our involvement in it.

The dynamics of consent, however, are not easily pinned down. We, and some of of our colleagues, have made various attempts to do this, using examples (such as debates in different countries over the siting of similar technological facilities) that clearly reflect very different patterns of influence by the three active biases (Thompson 1986a, Kunreuther, Linneroth *et al.* 1983, Brickman 1984). In Britain, for instance, hierarchies and markets have tended to be strong and equities weak. In the United States hierarchies have tended to be weak and both equities and markets strong. Wildavsky (1982) has taken a longitudinal look at American political life and has shown how egalitarians used to be able to get what they wanted by insisting that government remained small and left them alone ('American exceptionalism', as it is called). More recently (perhaps because government has got big and no longer leaves them alone) they have become more politically active, insisting that government intervene so as to decrease economic differences (act against the individualist position) and to equalize statuses (act against the hierarchical position).

At a more micro-level, Rayner (1986) has looked at the very different risk behaviours of surgeons, radiographers, plumbers and patients who (provided they all do their appropriate things, whilst to some extent respecting the rights of all the others) actually make a hospital function. He has shown how these groups map onto the cultural theory frame and how, when members of one group overstep some ill-defined but real enough line, consents are withdrawn and the whole pluralized *regime* is thrown into something of a crisis until such time as apologies are tendered, new procedures agreed, and ruffled feathers smoothed. Of course, we all know that this sort of thing happens all the time – that conflict helps us refine and reaffirm custom – but the plural rationalities framework gives us some useful insights into just how and why this happens and, more importantly, into how and why it sometimes goes wrong. We begin to see how the sporadic crises of hospital life prompt a continuous learning process by which the variously institutionalized actors discover (and continually rediscover) how to regulate their interactions in a way that gives considerable stability over time. Though they may not realize it, their regime (as Edmund Burke would have been pleased to point out) furnishes them with a *constitution* which, though it may well defy definition, is certainly capable of being perceived.

Both Rayner (1984) and MacLean (1986) have zeroed-in on this learning process and have isolated the various 'models of consent' that sound the alarm bells when the various lines have been overstepped, and that then provide the moral stances for the ensuing rumpus.

Models of consent

In the most extreme model – *direct consent* – a decision is justifiable only if everyone concerned accedes to that specific decision. This, as anyone who has ever attended one of their interminable meetings will know, is the egalitarians' model of consent. Such a model gives rise to what is called the method of expressed preferences: the only permissible basis for assessing a risk is each person's stated evaluation of that risk. The fact that the level of insurance premiums indicates that that risk is much lower, or the fact that he was chain-smoking untipped, high-tar cigarettes while pronouncing the risks of very low-level radiation to be unacceptably high, can have no bearing on the determination of direct consent.

In *implicit consent*, consent in one area is taken to justify a choice in another area. In this model, preferences are assumed to be consistent and transitive. This means that a single metric, 'willingness to pay', can be used to deduce consent in one area from the evident preparedness of a person to go along with some other risk in some other area. Of course, this assumes that going along with is the same thing as freely choosing but, once that assumption has been made, we get the method of revealed preferences that is so characteristic of the individualist (and of his clone, the neoclassical economist, who could not get his elegant theory off the ground if preferences were not consistent and transitive).

But, in *hypothetical consent*, even this tenuous link with the individual and his actual preferences is severed. In its place we find an idealization: an argument about what someone would consent to under certain specified conditions; conditions that may well be unrealized (and, indeed, unrealizable). The expert scientists of the British Ministry of Agriculture, Fisheries and Food, in declaring certain pesticides safe provided the specified procedures were followed – procedures that demonstrably could not be followed in the actual conditions under which spraying was caried out (Wynne 1989) – were clearly operating this model of consent. This model, in effect, insists that someone else knows better what a person's preferences should be. It is, therefore, the hierarchist's model. Since personal preferences have no place in this model, the method by which it is actually applied has to fasten on some extrapersonal ideal. 'Divine right', 'the Queen's pleasure' or 'the national interest' can be invoked here but, often enough, nature (the level of natural background radiation, for instance, as a standard by which to set acceptable levels for man-made radiation) is drawn upon to furnish this ideal. The figure 10^{-6}, which is now much bandied about in Britain as the acceptable level of risk, is an attempt to generalize the background risks we all live with.

Though these three complete the 'active' models of consent, they conceal, between them, a fourth 'passive' model: *non-consent*. Direct consent assumes that those who consent directly are sufficiently engaged socially to know their preferences; implicit consent assumes that if someone is bearing a particular level of risk it is because she

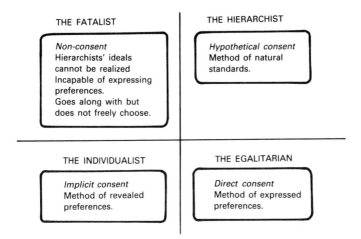

THE FATALIST

> Non-consent
> Hierarchists' ideals
> cannot be realized
> Incapable of expressing
> preferences.
> Goes along with but
> does not freely choose.

THE HIERARCHIST

> Hypothetical consent
> Method of natural
> standards.

THE INDIVIDUALIST

> Implicit consent
> Method of revealed
> preferences.

THE EGALITARIAN

> Direct consent
> Method of expressed
> preferences.

Figure 8.1 Models of consent, and the methods by which they are applied, mapped onto the political cultures.

has chosen to accept it, and hypothetical consent assumes that the idealized conditions it specifies can be met in practice. Those for whom these assumptions are not valid – the fatalists – pass straight through the meshes in the nets of all three models. Decisions are made for them, whether they consent or not (Figure 8.1). The method that accompanies each of these models of consent specifies what sort of data are to be taken into account: personal expressed preferences in direct consent, revealed preferences in implicit consent, and natural (or otherwise idealized) standards in hypothetical consent. In other words, each model, thanks to the distinctive 'rules of closure' by which it selects and organizes data for decision, defines what is and is not information.

Following up on this crucial connection between models of consent and definitions of information, Wynne and Otway (1982) and Thompson and Wildavsky (1986a) have looked at what happens to the supply of information in an organization that is culturally plural, and all organizations, they insist, *are* culturally plural. Large corporations, for instance, face outward towards markets, but internally more hierarchical relationships prevail (hence their current efforts to introduce a measure of 'intrapreneuring'). At lower levels (typing pools, for instance) things may become much more egalitarian and, of course, there are always some (the 'laterally promoted', for instance) who find themselves squeezed out to the fatalistic margins of it all.

The occupants of each of these organizational positions then define information in such a way as to promote their preferred way of life. Individualists shift the really vital decisions away from the formalized 'decision support system' and onto the 'old boy net'. Hierarchists stick loyally to the procedures that are enshrined in their 'management information system', blissfully unaware that those towards the bottom of the organization are feeding in and sifting out data according to the criteria appropriate to their egalitarian pattern of relations (Hirschmann and Lindblom 1970). Carried to its logical extreme (as it was on a highly successful Everest expedition) an 'overground leadership' ends up okaying the wishes of an 'underground leadership': the decisions are made at the bottom, and the top and bottom then join together in carrying them out (Thompson 1978). The only possible conclusion is that insurgency (creative if the interaction of the divergent parts carries the whole in an upward direction, destructive if it does not) is inevitable.

No single model of consent ever holds universal sway, no single method of determining acceptable risk is ever acceptable to all. No organization is ever as neat and uni-cultural as the organization chart in its chief executive's office suggests, no one way of organizing data for decision ever prevails over the others. No success, or failure, is ever unattended by insurgency. What eventually happens is not, and never could be, the clearly traceable consequence of some uniform and uniformly informed consent. It is, rather, the by-product of the endless struggle between the mutually incompatible models of consent, helped and hindered on its way by a nature that does not always bend itself so as to conform to the certainties that are proclaimed by the various political cultures.

Sir Edwin Landseer's grim painting of an ice-fast ship, hopelessly off course, its pluralized crew beset by polar bears – entitled 'Man Proposes, God Disposes'[6] – nicely depicts the sort of dead ends our inter-institutional decision making sometimes leads us into. Sometimes, of course, the complex chemistry works in a more creative direction, we triumphantly complete the North West Passage, and the polar bears go hungry. How can we get more of the second and less of the first?

The answer to this momentous question (an engineering question, if ever there was one!) lies in the learning process: in the constructive interplay of the contradictory certainties, the contradictory rules of closure, the contradictory information, and so on that accompany the four political cultures. The analyses we have given (of the lavatory rim-blocks, for instance, and of the energy debate) have taken us right into this fourfold interplay whilst still preserving its ineradicable inchoateness. And the informal constitutions of hospitals, the time-honoured fudges by which professions keep their churches broad enough to encompass within themselves enough of the variety that exists outside them, and the green-fingered skill by which a good manager harnesses the insurgency of those he manages (leading them, you might say, by being one of them and yet not being one of them) show us this learning process at its unconscious best. But, as the very existence of activities such as technology assessment and of prescriptive frameworks like decision theory and cost–benefit analysis confirms, many people are not prepared to leave our learning process in this unconscious state. They wish it to be conscious.

Unfortunately, they have assumed that because it is not conscious it is not there. They have then set about providing it from scratch: a disastrous venture that is the equivalent of doctors designing an artificial digestive system, and implanting it in the human body, once they realize that we do not consciously digest our food. Our argument, by contrast, is that this conscious learning process should be put together from a careful and humble probing of the unconscious processes that are already in place. That, in a nutshell, is what we have been doing throughout this book, and the point it has now brought us to is the dynamics of consent.

We can now see how the four political cultures, thanks to their models of consent and their attendant informations and rules of closure, generate these dynamics: their shifting coalitions, their technological constraints (once resources have been irretrievably sunk into one preferred way of doing things rather than another) and their eternally inchoate evaluations. We can also see how extraordinarily complex and unpredictable these dynamics can become, especially when (as we must) we introduce nature's erratic vetoes: the pack-ice and the polar bears. The task now is to find out exactly what the implications of all this are for these conscious efforts that are currently being made.

Notes

1. Linking two rivers in Lancashire, England. Methane, which had accumulated in the system, exploded in the pumping station with great loss of life.

2. We use this word in the sense that recent technological developments (such as the growing role of computing, telecommunications and micro-electronics) give rise to questions about new social circumstances and create new social, political and cultural challenges (Lyons 1988).

3. In many Western industrialized countries, another such dynamic can now be clearly seen in the case of growing consumer demand for health food products (additive-free, pesticide-free, etc.) and the subsequent response of food companies.

4. Nor are they as good as the best human experts, or ever likely to be (Dreyfus 1985).

5. It is, of course, because of this interwoven quality that our arguments concern the *nature* of technology as a social process, rather than an attempt to define 'technology' as an entity in the conventional sense. We agree with the historian Hughes when he says: 'technology can be defined no more easily than politics. Rarely do we ask for a definition of politics. To ask for *the* definition of technology is to be equally innocent of complex reality' (Hughes 1989:5).

6. This painting hangs in the Great Hall of the Royal Holloway and Bedford New College, University of London. It has to be covered with a cloth when the hall is used for examinations.

Chapter 9

Deconstructing Technology (And Putting the Pieces Together Again)

T he main thrust of our argument has been that the substantive core that has provided the theoretical basis for the study of technological decision making, does not exist. What does exist, we have shown, is a plurality (but not an infinitude) of contending and contradictory problem definitions. That this is the case is increasingly being realized, both by those who study this important aspect of our lives together and by those who are charged with making the decisions. In other words, the need to switch from the substantive core assumption to the plural definitions assumption is now quite well recognized at the empirical and practical levels. The trouble, however, is that the theory is still stuck with the invalid assumption. Unsticking it, and then moving it across onto the valid assumption, has been our aim in developing our cultural theory. Since practice has got so far ahead of theory, we can best explore the implications of this cultural theory by choosing as our point of departure the most advanced instance of practice that has come to our attention: the *sociale kaart* (TNO 1984, Smits *et al.* 1987).

The *sociale kaart* ('social map') is a typically Dutch response to a typically Dutch predicament: a densely populated and heavily industrialized country in which the widely polarized views on technology and its social and environmental concomitants translate very directly (thanks to an electoral system of proportional representation) into the political process. Dutch society, like others in Western Europe, is many-pillared but it is unique in having very little by way of an integrating pediment to tie all these structural supports together. Its mediating institutions of government are simply no match for all the divergences and contradictions in the assessment of technological development that sprout up from the grassroots. In consequence, the fudges, the trade-offs, the brush-offs and the partisan mutual adjustments, that in most European countries manage somehow to transform this Tower of Babel into something that looks like a temple of social choice, leave the Dutch view from the top much the same as it is from the bottom.[1] Does this divergence from the European norm suggest that things have gone seriously awry in Holland or does it suggest that the Dutch are evolving a distinctive, but still viable, way of doing things? Are they sinking beneath their post-industrial heritage or responding creatively to a fortuitous stimulus?

Since the substantive core, if present, would allow those who had access to it to bang all these divergent Dutch heads together and force them into some sort of line, the *sociale kaart* is a repugnant device to those whose faith in that substantive core is still unshaken. But we see it all in a much more favourable light.

The Dutch, we say, lead the world in multiple problem definitions. Looking on the bright side, they also lead the world in multiply-defined solutions, and the *sociale kaart* represents their first explicit attempt to harness this remarkable resource. Laid out on this 'social map' we see all the interested parties clearly differentiated, not just in terms of their interests in relation to some particular development but also in terms of their perceptions of what that development *is*. Unable to force the policy actors into a single definitional mould, the Dutch propose instead to institutionalize this map of how far apart they all are and then to try to use it as a major input to their decision-making process. So we can open up the implications of our cultural theory by showing how it transforms this pig's ear of a proposal (when seen from the conventional theoretical position) into a silk purse for policy choice in the plural mode.

Two Kinds of Decision Making

Problem solving is a social activity. It is not the problem itself but the relationship between the problem and those who are engaged in solving it that we must try to understand. Sometimes all those involved have essentially the same understanding of what the problem is; sometimes they do not. Sometimes there is but a single problem definition because those who subscribe to that definition have managed to get rid of those who do not; sometimes there are plural problem definitions because no one set of protagonists has, up till now, managed to get rid of the rest. So a single problem definition should always be approached with caution. Before we rush to solve it we should pause and look around to see whether those who are organized around that definition are actively excluding others who subscribe to other, contradictory, definitions. This is not to deny that some problems may be purely technical; only that, often enough, they are political as well. And, of course, one of the shrewdest political moves in the book is to get *your* problem labelled 'technical'. That simultaneously gets rid of any contending versions of the problem and de-politicizes yours!

In the conventional practice of technology assessment, however, the problems are all technical and the perceived task is to solve them. The student of political culture has to start from further back. He has first to ask himself how all these technical problems *became* technical problems. He has to treat the practice of technology assessment as a political activity. Risk assessment, too, runs into these same political difficulties whenever it encounters divergent perceptions. The trouble, as we have seen, is that risk perception is not something that can simply be tacked onto quantitative risk analysis as a humanizing refinement. Before risks can be analyzed they have to be perceived, and if different groups perceive different risks (and perceive the level and acceptability of the same risks differently), then those perceptions are inevitably prior to any formalized business of assessment. To arbitrarily select one, and to label all the others 'misperceptions' is simply to act politically under the misapprehension (or deliberate pretence) that you are acting scientifically. So the first practical implication of cultural theory follows directly from its revelation of this pitfall. It alerts us to the desirability of not falling into it.

The traditional conceptualization of technology assessment (with its focus on the 'factual' impacts) cannot be synthesized with political culture. Technology assessment is justified by its claim to scientific objectivity; political culture denies it that claim. Yet, it is our argument that, despite their fundamental incompatibility, each is still valid *under certain circumstances*. The practical challenge lies not in choosing one or the other but in our learning to discriminate between circumstances so as to know when to apply which.

If, as sometimes happens, the problems *are* just technical then what we have is the familiar *decision making under uncertainty*. But if the problems are political as well, then we are dealing with a completely different animal: *decision making under contradictory certainties* (Thompson and Warburton 1985). Our argument is simply that what is conventionally termed 'technological decision making' is not at all an homogeneous kind of problem solving. It straddles both kinds of decision making yet is incapable of distinguishing between them; it lacks the requisite variety. What we have to do, therefore, is, first, to develop a more variegated approach that is capable of distinguishing between these two kinds of decision making and, second, to derive from that approach some simple 'selection rules' (or 'indicators') that will tell us just where and when technological risks are best handled by formalized and 'neutral' techniques (such as risk assessment and cost–benefit analysis) and just where and when it becomes imperative to take their political and social contexts into explicit account.

A cultural basis for discrimination

The cultural analysis, as advanced in this book, starts from the recognition that the actual risks associated with a particular technology are not always directly accessible. That is not to say that the risks we do associate with a technology are just in the mind; only that they are socially selected and likely, therefore, to be perceived differently by different policy actors. The different energy futures, for instance, or the different dose–response curves, or the different oil and gas reserve estimates, or the different convictions as to what paradichlorobenzene will do to us once it has got itself into the water cycle, are all perfectly feasible, given the wide uncertainty that currently surrounds all these issues. They are examples of structural uncertainty, something that is quite different from the more familiar notion of technical uncertainty.

In the case of technical uncertainty or imprecision (Wynne 1987) we find broad agreement among the experts that the uncertainty exists and that, given the present state of knowledge, they cannot say exactly what the risk is. However, what they can do is reach some agreement on the scale of the uncertainty: they can agree to a figure that is qualified by agreed uncertainty bounds. But in structural uncertainty the reverse applies. Each expert knows within narrow limits what the risks are but, when we try to aggregate those certainties, we find no common core of agreement. Instead, as we have seen, they fall into a number of 'certainty clumps', each of which contradicts the certainties of all the others. Far from the agreed and *tunable* understanding of the problem that we get with technical uncertainty, the debates that are characterized by contradictory certainties are essentially *untunable*. Each policy actor – and each expert – is free, as it were, to choose what he would like the facts to be. The available data, in other words, do not suggest a single credible and unequivocal picture of what is going on.[2] Such a picture can only be obtained by arbitrarily declaring some of the data to be anomalous.

Cultural theory makes sense out of what is going on by treating these declarations – these value-determined selections of fact – as the conceptual means by which the structural divergences may be identified. The cultural perspective emphasizes that these 'arbitrary' declarations and 'free' choices of fact are structural. They are not so much conscious and voluntary decisions on the part of each policy actor as decisions that are supplied to him, in the form of unquestioned and self-evident assumptions, by the institutions in which he happens to be embedded. But, when we look at each of the various policy actors on the *sociale kaart*, these deep divergences are not directly revealed to us. It is here, therefore, that we need to turn to cultural analysis. Cultural theory, in effect, deconstructs these largely unconscious and involuntary decision biases. It enables us to examine the mutually sustaining relationships between the various sets of certainties, information and rules of closure among policy actors and the various institutional settings that define each policy actor and his distinctive stance and, in so doing, actually put him onto the *sociale kaart*. At the same time, cultural analysis alerts us to the possibility that other institutionally induced certainties, thanks to the essentially political nature of the arena, may have been denied a place on the *sociale kaart*.

So the *sociale kaart* (as formulated in the context of recent Dutch policy discussions on technology assessment[3]) is certainly a major advance on the conventional single problem/single solution approach (the adversarial mode) that simply demands to know which definition is the 'correct' definition. It rightly grants legitimacy to all those who can get themselves onto the map, and it takes account of their respective problem definitions, interests and values. In so doing, it institutionalizes the exploratory mode and radically shifts the criteria for policy choice and technology assessment away from optimality and towards viability. But, despite these valuable advances, the *sociale kaart*, as presently conceived, still does not go to the heart of the decision process it seeks to improve. It maps only *some* of the policy actors, and it maps them in terms of their *given* interests. The contribution of cultural theory, by contrast, is that it enables us to get at the underlying processses by which actors climb onto, or are pushed off, the *sociale kaart*. It goes to the very inner core of politics: the institutional *origins* of the divergent preferences, interests and strategies. The *sociale kaart*, if we may risk a bilingual pun, has been placed in front of the cultural horse. What happens when we put them the other way round?.

The cultural overlay

Cultural theory, as we have seen, sets up a fourfold scheme of cultural pluralism, based on four distinct social contexts and their concomitant moral commitments and strategies. It is a pluralism, moreover, that is *essential*, in the sense that each cultural bias – towards market solutions, towards hierarchical solutions, towards egalitarian solutions, and towards fatalistic acceptance – is not viable on its own. Individualists, for instance, need the hierarchists to enforce the law of contract, the hierarchists need the fatalists to sit on top of, the egalitarians need the inegalitarian excesses of the individualists and the hierarchists to criticize, and so on.

So this notion of an essential, but strictly limited, cultural pluralism can be used as a conceptual tool for recognizing the divergences in social assessment – of technologies and policies – by those who make up the arena in which our technologies (along with everything else that makes our social world go round) are hammered out. We can visualize this fourfold scheme as a cultural overlay that can be superimposed on the *sociale kaart* so as to provide a deep explanation of where all the features on that map come from (and to alert us to the possibility that some may have been excluded). Our central argument is that, whenever a policy debate is characterized not just by technical uncertainty but by structural uncertainty as well, we should analyze it in terms of this cultural overlay.[4]

Although this fourfold scheme, with its plural risks, its plural resources and its plural rationalities, is our cultural overlay, we must stress that it should not be seen as some kind of ingenious tool (or decision aid) for generating multi-attribute utility functions, loser compensation estimates, multilateral trade-offs, conflict resolutions and the like. Rather, we see it as a way of resisting all these sorts of superficial and patronizing fixes and of redirecting concern over technology assessment and policy towards the plight of some of the most fundamental institutions of the modern state: institutions whose credibility is currently being eroded precisely because structural uncertainties are being treated as if they are merely technical.

What Should We Do With Technology Assessment?

Since technology assessment is already with us, we have two options. We can discard it and start again from scratch, or we can modify it until it functions more sensibly. Since we have already argued that technology assessment is a perfectly valid procedure whenever the uncertainties are only technical, we favour the second of these options. But, in order to explain the modifications that are needed, we must first summarize cultural theory's interpretation of the whole process that this modified technology assessment will try to improve.

Suppose a new technological development occurs: larger turbine generators, say, or higher-capacity power lines, or taller flues. Without knowing much about it (and, as Collingridge (1980) reminds us so forcibly, at the early stages of the development process no one *can* know much about it) those who identify with each cultural bias can guess whether the effect will be to increase or decrease social distinctions, to impose, avoid or reject authority. These guesses are made more definite by observing what like-minded individuals do (and what *un*like-minded individuals do). It does not take much, for example, for members of individualist or egalitarian political cultures to figure out whether they approve of the centralization of electricity supply, or for the members of a hierarchical political culture to surmise that its centralized control is better than its fragmentation.

Of course people may be, and often are, mistaken. There are unanticipated consequences (acid rain, for instance) and there are inconsequent anticipations (catastrophic collapse as a result of planes flying into the Empire State Building, for instance).[5] To seek is not necessarily to find a culturally rational course of action. Unanticipated consequences, therefore, become new developments and, in their turn, are supported or opposed. Inconsequent anticipations, likewise, can be pounced upon, or quietly forgotten about, according to how they measure up to the various criteria that are integral to each of the cultural biases. To be culturally rational is the intention, not necessarily the accomplishment, and it is this time-lagged mismatch that turns technology policy into an historical *process* and us into its 'prisoners'. And, finally, it is precisely this inescapable 'imprisonment' that makes the whole learning process endless.

If we buy this account of how life goes on then we also buy the following: technologies, like everything else that develops as a result of social processes, are in perpetual assessment, perpetual *cultural* assessment. If technology, by virtue of its social nature, is nothing other than the output of this perpetual assessment process then what on earth is this thing called technology assessment? Whatever it is, it is not what it conventionally is claimed to be: a method for socially assessing something that is, until that moment, unassessed. In other words, technology assessment has been founded on a serious misunderstanding of what technology *is*. Far from being socially unassessed, technology is nothing other than the *product* of social assessment.

Of course, not all the social beings enjoy equal access to the development process at all times. Some may be largely excluded in the early stages with the result that later, when they do gain access, they set in its path obstacles that cannot be surmounted. In these instances, the development process has set off along a path that turns out to be unsustainable. This, for instance, is what happened to the paradichlorobenzene and the moulding technology for the lavatory rim-blocks, forcing a jump out of that trajectory and into a more sustainable one. In the rim-blocks' case the jump was not too painful, but sometimes (as with the nuclear power station at Zwentendorf, in Austria) it can be very costly.

In this view, technological development is an inherently hit-and-miss affair – like rural development (Thompson *et al.* 1986) and urban development (Thompson 1987) – in which no single cultural bias ever has a clear run for long. What we end up with is always the product of an untidy process of *bricolage*, never of an immaculate, surprise-free, and fully specified scheme.

Once we start to see technological development in this way we may be tempted to try to modify technology assessment so that it takes account of the fact that what it is assessing is already the product of these sorts of contending cultural assessments. Its aim would then be to anticipate the various obstacles, and thereby to steer developments away from the unsustainable paths and onto the sustainable ones. Since sustainability has to be both social *and* physical (the crew *and* the pack ice) this kind of technology assessment will become possible only if we can come up with some criteria for judging whether or not a particular development path is likely to be sustainable. But (and this really is the end of the road for the sort of hubristic technology assessment we have become used to) each cultural bias already claims to do precisely that, and we already have all sorts of institutional arrangements – we call them democracy – designed (sometimes deliberately, sometimes by happy accident, and often none too perfectly) to mediate between the many contradictory assessments that they come up with.

So what does this corrected, and perhaps alarming, understanding of technology as something embedded in social life, rather than something outside that has impacts on it, suggest we should be doing? It suggests three things. First, that we look to our mediating institutions: their inadequacies and their irrelevancies, their design and their redesign. Second, that we look into the life cycles of specific technological developments (the rim-blocks, for instance) and ask ourselves some hard and general questions about sustainability: what, if anything, can we do to distinguish between those paths that will be sustainable and those that will not? Third, that we think about flexibility; about how to minimize path commitment; about what we can do to cope with the obstacles to sustainability when we cannot anticipate them. These three foci define the sort of humble (and design process oriented) technology assessment that we would like to see developed. They also help us to clarify the sorts of circumstances in which the old style of technology assessment is still valid.

Selection rules for decision modes: What kind of technology assessment?

Cultural theory does not explain everything, nor do we need to call on cultural analysis every time a decision has to be made about technology. The theory comes into its own only when we have a persistently polarized debate, and we only need to call for the cultural analysis when we hear the ominous clash of contradictory certainties. So how, in practice, can we tell when to wheel up the cultural apparatus and when to wheel up a more conventional kind of technology assessment?

The conventional apparatus, we would argue, is appropriate whenever the uncertainties are just technical; the cultural apparatus is appropriate whenever the uncertainties are structural as well. And of course, even when they *are* structural, it is still quite appropriate for each 'certainty clump' to carry out its own formalized risk assessment with its term of reference set out according to its own definition of the problem. Each of these assessments would then have its legitimacy guaranteed by the *sociale kaart* (and its cultural overlay) and would then be able to feed its two-penn'orth into the institutionalized processes of decision. Since such assessments require considerable resources, and since the various policy actors are seldom equally endowed with resources, this consideration of the purely technical barriers to plural assessment takes us straight into some of the important questions of *institutional design*. For instance:

- How can we ensure greater equality in research funding and access to information among the various groups on the *sociale kaart*?
- How can we modify our governmental institutions (not to mention our professions and our corporations) to enable us to cope more effectively with plural problem definitions and culturally divergent technology assessments?
- How can we avoid relegating decisions over technology to specialized agencies and expert groups, in the mistaken belief that we are handing over merely technical problems, in cases where the questions have such a high political content?
- How can we optimize the 'input' and 'feedback' from those on the *sociale kaart* into decision-making institutions so as to help us recognize what assessment mode is appropriate?

Each of these specific questions has us teetering on the edge of the great pitfall in policy analysis and institutional design: the 'arbitrary' selection of just one of the culturally valid positions. Grossly unequal endowments and excessive secrecy will keep some problem definitions off the *sociale kaart* and outside the debate. Over-formalized inquiry procedures, or too narrowly defined risk measurements, will deny 'standing' to some of the cultural biases. The entrusting of political tasks to bureaucratic bodies (that then have to treat them as merely technical) will lead to far too tidy and private an arena of policy actors and positions. All this suggests that, once we have made a few of these sorts of modifications, the institutions themselves will then be able to tell us which decision mode we should adopt. This, after all, is not so surprising a conclusion. If, as we have been arguing, the tacit wisdom is already there, 'internalized' in the various mediating institutions, then it is only a matter of designing the channels by which they can communicate that wisdom and thereby make it more explicit.

If only one risk assessment is called for then (as long as we have made sure that our institutional procedures cannot be captured by just one cultural bias[6]) we know that only technical uncertainty is involved. If more than one risk assessment is called for then we know that there is structural uncertainty as well. Mediating institutions, we are arguing, should be designed (or redesigned) so that they always contain the requisite variety; and that is exactly what the *sociale kaart*, once it is institutionalized and fitted with its cultural overlay, can do. This cultural overlay helps us make sure that some of the policy actors do not find themselves pushed off the *sociale kaart* by the others. It guards against the all-too-common situation in which the formal TA process ends up being captured by just a single cultural perspective (or by a too-cosy alliance between just two cultural biases; the 'energy orthodoxy' of the 1960s and 70s, for instance, in which the hierarchists and the individualists, through their shared commitment to economic growth and to large-scale production units, effectively excluded the egalitarians whose commitments were the reverse of these). Of course, just because all the cultural biases are represented on the *sociale kaart* it does not follow that the technology will go off down the best possible developmental path. The biases, once their access to the decision process has been ensured, have to interact in a constructive manner (as they did in the case of the lavatory rim-blocks). However, the first essential is to ensure that all the biases have access. If they do not then it is extremely unlikely that the technology will be steered along a viable path.

The development of nuclear power, for instance, especially during its early and most innovative phase, has been dominated by a single cultural bias – the hierarchical – and institutionally insulated both from the criticism of the egalitarians and from the discipline of the marketplace. This entrenchment has been world wide but is, perhaps, most marked in Britain where nuclear power has remained the exclusive preserve of a tightly knit expert community whose stability has for too long (it is changing now, thanks to the privatization of the electricity industry) been guaranteed by the single-mission organization that was created at the end of the Second World War specifically to harness the power of the atom to peaceful ends (Wynne 1982).

Although people have tended to assume that the nuclear technology we now have is the way it is because of the physical properties of the atoms it seeks to harness, there is no doubt that it could have gone down some remarkably different paths (modular, mass-produced and quite small-scale 'walk-away' reactors, for instance) had the appropriate nudges been given, at the appropriate moments, by the appropriate cultural biases. Had that happened (that is, had the decision process not been captured by just one cultural bias) the present obstacles to viability, both at the operational level of implementation[7] and in terms of social acceptance, might never have arisen. If, as is possible, these obstacles are unavoidable, whichever path nuclear power might have taken, then that knowledge would have been available very much sooner. Either outcome – finding the sustainable path or finding out that there isn't one – would have been vastly superior to what has in fact happened. The practical message of cultural theory is that, though the entrenchment of technologies is inevitable, their entrenchment along unviable lines of development is not.

This view of things, a view that is very different from, and much more modest than, that held by the inventors of TA, is implicitly acknowledged in recent attempts (by the same people who gave us the *sociale kaart*, the Dutch)[8] to formulate strategies for constructive technology assessment (CTA). In CTA the modest aim is to devise some ways of influencing the interactions that constitute the process of technological development so that more of them are constructive and fewer of them are destructive. Since cultural theory provides us with a complete typology of possible interactions (that is, it tells us what there is, or could be, to interact with what) it meshes nicely with the aims of CTA. Indeed, it actually makes CTA *usable*. A constructive approach to technology assessment, cultural theory tells us, has to be based on an understanding of the social character of the technology process: a process that is continually driven by the contention of the four cultural biases (specifically, the contradictory technology assessments that each of them is all the time making and their divergent definitions of what the technology itself is).

But to say that technology is a social process is not to say that the 'hardware' (the plant, the nuts and bolts, the physical equipment) can take on any shape that is socially desired. Nuclear technology could have gone down more than one path but it could not have gone down any path. That which is socially desirable cannot be achieved if it is physically impossible. This warns us, first, that the interactions we wish to make more constructive are remarkably complex and subtle and, second, that since we are an essential part of those interactions we can never stand right outside them, as it were, to assess them (which, of course is what TA set out to do). The adherents of each political culture are doing everything they can both to steer technological developments in the direction they see as most desirable, and to put as many obstacles as possible in the way of those who are trying to steer things in directions that they see as being most desirable. To a considerable extent they promote these two linked aims by appealing to their contradictory convictions as to what is physically possible. They are able to do this (that is, they are able to muster credibility) because enough of the crucial physical facts are inchoate; insufficiently formed to be able to do what we expect facts to do – speak for themselves. But, inchoate or not, nature does have some vetoes, some points at which she steps in and says 'no', and these vetoes raise a further set of obstacles in the paths down which the various political cultures are trying to get the technologies to go.

That these two sets of obstacles (the socially placed and the naturally placed) will be there is the first thing that cultural theory tells us. The second thing it tells us is that, thanks to the essentially inchoate nature of so much of the process, we will never be able to distinguish between them (those whose myth of nature predicts an obstacle's presence will insist that it is natural; those whose myth predicts its absence will insist that their opponents put it there. The history of nuclear power, for instance, is littered with these sorts of irresoluble disagreements). All we can say with certainty is, first, that the dynamics of technology do involve necessary paths (*chreods*, as they are sometimes called) down which, from time to time, technological developments must go regardless of organizational commitments and, second, that people and organizations (and the cultural biases that keep those people organized in one or other of a small number of viable ways) must always remain the 'supporting medium' for the development of technologies and their application. Technology, in other words, is a dynamic and evolutionary process that is only possible if patterns of *things* (technological chreods) are accompanied by patterns of *people* (ways of organizing and disorganizing) and patterns of *ideas* (cultural biases).

This as yet under-explored model of technology dynamics, a model in which what is happening in one corner (or even in two corners) of the things–people–ideas triangle is never enough to explain the development of the whole, provides the deep conceptual basis for the practice of constructive technology assessment. And the *sociale kaart*, once it has been fitted with its cultural overlay, is the tool by which we can capture this process without at the same time subordinating any of its vital components – things, people and ideas – to the others.

This tool, in drawing our attention to the divergent institutional assessments of technologies that the adherents of the various cultural biases are making, sensitizes us to the interactions that they are all the time engaged in. Constructive technology assessment, we can now see, is something of a misnomer. What we are trying to institutionalize through the *sociale kaart* and its cultural overlay is, rather, a framework for encouraging the more constructive interplay of the technology assessments that are *already there* and without which technology itself would not be possible. From now on, when we speak of CTA, it is this framework that we have in mind.

CTA in Action

The first 'rule' of this modified CTA is that the more political cultures have access to the development process the more chance there is of it not becoming unviably entrenched. This, of course, is the justification for ensuring that funds and institutional support are available for multiple formal risk assessments, each starting from its distinct perception of what is risky and its distinctive definition of what the technology is. The second 'rule' is that this multiplication should be strictly limited to the number of socially viable positions on the cultural overlay. Risk assessments should be multiple but parsimonious: they should not be multiplied beyond necessity.

Having recognized and respected these various actors, the practitioners of CTA then have to determine the limits of that respect. For instance, a policy actor who insists that the dose–response curve at low levels of exposure is linear should be respected (as too should the actor who insists that it is quadratic, and the actor who insists that it is parabolic), but an actor who insists that it is quadratic (or parabolic) at high exposures should not be respected. The reason is that, in moving from low to high exposures, we have moved out of the inchoate and into the choate. We have gone from a region of structural uncertainty (within which contradictory certainties are valid) to one of technical uncertainty (within which contradictory certainties are not valid). If we are to guard against treating structural uncertainty as if it were technical uncertainty (and that, we have been arguing, is what we must do if our interventions are not to be destructive) then we will have to have an effective means of distinguishing between them.

All sorts of quite easy-to-read signs can tell us which sort of uncertainty we are dealing with. *Overspill* (those debates that quickly go beyond their purported technical confines and fuse with others; nuclear power and the extension to Frankfurt airport, for example) is a clear, but rather late, indicator of structural uncertainty. Persistent expert disagreement, as we have seen, is another. But it should also be possible, by drawing on the various predictions that cultural theory makes (all the rows of Table 5.1) to come up with some much earlier indicators. The different engineering aesthetics, for instance, could have alerted the multinational to the likelihood of Green opposition to its rim-blocks long before it reached the point of actually launching them on the market. In much the same way, the predictions as to which sorts of risks will gain salience in each of the cultural biases (for instance, the long-term radiation risks inherent in nuclear power that so exercise the egalitarians, and the contract security risks associated with the trans-oceanic transport of liquefied natural gas that loom so large for the individualists) can set the alarm-bells ringing even when a technology is little more than a 'randy glint of anticipation in its parent's eye' (Wynne 1985).

Indeed, since there is scarcely a disaster that befalls us that has not been predicted by someone, somewhere, it should be perfectly feasible to institute a *risk register* in which all these warnings can be assembled and gradually sorted out into 'Cassandra' and 'cry wolf' files. In this way, the unanticipated consequences and the inconsequent anticipations of all the cultural biases could be harnessed to the realistic task of minimizing the entrenchment of technology. We could also set about connecting this risk register to the physical and organizational indicators of inflexibility that have been developed by Collingridge and James (personal communication), but it is time for us to call a halt.

Our aim in this book, we should remind ourselves, has been to bring the theory of politics, technology and social choice within hailing distance of the practitioners – the politicians, the engineers and the citizens – and this we have now done. Where theory and practice go, now that they can communicate with one another once more, is a different story; one that would (and, we suspect, will) fill another book.

Notes

1. As can be seen, for example, in the case of Dutch environmental politics, where environmental groups play a considerable role in the formulation

of government policy. The Netherlands was the only country where the government organized a 'broad societal debate' on energy and the future of nuclear power (Turney and Schwarz 1983).

2. The process of social definition and negotiation about what constitutes certain and uncertain knowledge is particularly important in the context of political decision making. For an examination of the political sociology of the adequacy of knowledge, see Campbell (1985).

3. These discussions, begun in the early 1980s, have stressed that one of the main questions in technology assessment should be to find out what the *sociale kaart* looks like.

> Which individuals, groups and/or organizations are (or soon will be) affected by the technology? What sort of effects does the development have on those involved (interests, views)? Is there anything that can be said at the present time about future changes in this social map, which may, for example, be brought about by changes in sets of values, causes, or by the fact that new technological possibilities lead to new people becoming involved? (Smits *et al.* 1987:22).

4. And, as Wynne (1987) has pointed out, what in the conventional approach is taken to be purely technical imprecision, frequently turns out to be structural uncertainty or latent conflict between divergent problem frames.

5. Inconsequent, in this particular case, not because it has not happened yet but because a plane did fly into the building but did not cause it to collapse. It punched a neat plane-shaped hole in the steel-framed structure that was easily repaired.

6. Whether we can ever be sure of that is, of course, a big question. Cultural theory (with its fourfold requisite variety) and an institutionalized explanatory mode, at least allow us to try.

7. The accident at Three Mile Island has illustrated how the lack of participation by operators, in setting the design and operating features, proved the technology to be unviable at the level of implementation. The technology failed, because, as Wynne has put it, 'somewhere in the labyrinth of its enactment, people have not acted according to the designer's unrealistic assumptions and faiths' (Wynne 1983:23).

8. The idea of constructive technology assessment is being actively promoted by the Netherlands Organization for Technology Assessment.

Bibliography

Ackerman, B.A., Rose-Ackerman, S., Sawyer, J.W. and Henderson, D.W. (1974) *The Uncertain Search for Environmental Quality* (New York: Free Press).

Almond, G.A. and Verba, S. (1965) *The Civic Culture: Political Attitudes and Democracy in Five Nations* (Princeton, NJ: Princeton University Press).

Arrow, K.J. (1954) *Social Choice and Individual Values* 2nd edn (New York: Wiley).

Arthur, W.B. (1985) *Competing Technologies and Lock-in by Historical Small Events: The Dynamics of Allocation Under Increasing Returns*, Stanford, CEPR Publication No. 43 (revised edn).

Barnes, B. (1974) *Scientific Knowledge and Sociological Theory* (London: Routledge and Kegan Paul).

Barnes, B. and Edge, D. (eds) (1982) *Science in Context: Readings in the Sociology of Science* (Milton Keynes: Open University Press).

Benedict, R. (1935) *Patterns of Culture* (Boston: Houghton Mifflin).

Bentley, A. (1949) *The Process of Government* (Evanston, IL: Principa Press).

Benveniste, G. (1972) *The Politics of Expertise* (Berkley, CA: Glendossary Press).

Berg, M. (1975) 'The politics of technology assessment', *Journal of the International Society for Technology Assessment*, 1.

Berger, P. and Luckmann, T. (1967) *The Social Construction of Reality* (New York: Doubleday).

Bernstein, B. (1971, 1973, 1975) *Class, Codes and Controls: I, II, III* (London: Routledge and Kegan Paul).

Bijker, W.E., Hughes, T.P., and Pinch, T.J. (1987) *The Social Construction of Technological Systems* (Cambridge, MA: MIT Press).

Braybrooke, D. and Lindblom, C.E. (1963) *A Strategy of Decision* (Glencoe, IL: Free Press).

Brickman, R. (1984) 'Science and the politics of toxic chemicals regulations:

US and European contrasts', *Science, Technology and Human Values,* 9: 107–11.

Brooks, H. (1984) 'The resolution of technically intensive public policy disputes', *Science, Technology and Human Values,* 9: 39–50.

Brown, J. (ed) (1989) *Environmental Threats: Perception, Analysis and Management* (London/New York: Belhaven).

Campbell, B.L. (1982) *Disputes Among Experts: A Sociological Case Study of the Debate Over Biology in the MacKenzie Pipeline Inquiry,* PhD Thesis, McMaster University, Hamilton, Ontario, Canada.

Campbell, B.L. (1985) 'Uncertainty as symbolic action in disputes among experts', *Social Studies of Science,* 15: 429–53.

Caneva, K. (1981) 'What should we do with the monster? Electromagnetism and the psychosociology of knowledge' in E. Mendelsohn and Y. Elkana (eds) *Sciences and Cultures: Anthropological and Historical Studies of the Sciences. Sociology of the Sciences Yearbook 1981* (Dordrecht: Reidel).

Carley, M. (1981) *Rational Techniques in Policy Analysis* (London: Heinemann Educational).

Chapman, P. (1975) *Fuel's Paradise: Energy Options for Britain* (Harmondsworth: Penguin).

Chilver, H. (1975) 'Wider implications of catastrophe theory', *Nature,* 254.

Clark, W.C. (1980) 'Witches, floods and wonder drugs: Historical perspectives on risk management', in R.C. Schwing and W.A. Albers, Jr. (eds) *Societal Risk Assessment: How Safe Is Safe Enough?* (New York: Plenum).

Clark, W.C. and Munn, R.E. (eds) (1986) *Sustainable Development of the Biosphere* (Cambridge: Cambridge University Press).

Coates, V.T. and Fabian, T. (1982) 'Technology assessment in Europe and Japan', *Technological Forecasting and Social Change,* 22: 343–61.

Cochran, C.E. (1971). *The Politics of Interest: The Eclipse of Community in Contemporary Political Theory,* PhD Thesis, Duke University, Durham, North Carolina.

Cochran, C.E. (1973) 'The politics of interest: Philosophy and the limitations of the science of politics', *American Journal of Political Science,* 17: 745–66.

Cohen, J.L. (1981) 'Can human irrationality be experimentally demonstrated?' *Behavioural and Brain Sciences,* 4.

Collingridge, D. (1980) *The Social Control of Technology* (Milton Keynes: Open University Press).

Conrad, J. (ed) (1980) *Society, Technology and Risk Assessment* (London: Academic Press).

Cotgrove, S. (1982) *Catastrophe or Cornucopia: The Environment, Politics and the Future* (Chichester: Wiley).

Covello, V.T. (1983) 'The perception of technological risks: A literature review', *Technological Forecasting and Social Change,* 23: 285–97.

Critchley, O.H. (1978) *Aspects of the Historical, Philosophical and Mathematical Background to the Management of Nuclear Power Plants in the United Kingdom: Radiation Protection in Nuclear Power Plants and the Fuel Cycle* (London: British Nuclear Energy Society).

Cutt, J. (1975) 'Policy analysis: A conceptual base for a theory of improvement', *Policy Sciences*, 6: 223–98.

Dahl, R.A. and Lindblom, C.E. (1965) *Politics, Economics and Welfare* (New York: Harper).

Davis, J.S. (1987) 'Designing the future: Utopien als Notwendigkeit', in L. Burckhardt (ed), *Design der Zukunft* (Berlin: Dumont).

Dean, B. (1981) *The Peripheral Nature of Scientific and Technological Controversy in Federal Policy Formation*, Background Study No. 46 (Ottawa: Science Council of Canada).

Del Sesto, S.L. (1983) 'Uses of knowledge and values in technical controversies: The case of nuclear reactor safety in the US', *Social Studies of Science*, 13: 395–416.

Dickson, D. (1984) *The New Politics of Science* (New York: Pantheon).

Dierkes, M., Edwards, S. and Coppock, R. (eds) (1980) *Technological Risk: Its Perception and Handling in the European Community* (Cambridge, MA: Oelgeschlager, Gunn and Hain).

Dosi, G. (1982) 'Technological paradigms and technological trajectories', *Research Policy*, 11: 147–62.

Douglas, M. (1970) *Natural Symbols: Explorations in Cosmology* (Harmondsworth: Penguin).

Douglas, M. (1975) *Implicit Meanings* (London: Routledge and Kegan Paul).

Douglas, M. (1978) *Cultural Bias*, Occasional Paper No. 35 (London: Royal Anthropological Institute of Great Britain and Ireland).

Douglas, M. (1982) *Essays in the Sociology of Perception* (London: Routledge and Kegan Paul).

Douglas, M. (1985) *Risk Acceptability According to the Social Sciences* (New York: Russell Sage Foundation).

Douglas, M. (1986) *How Institutions Think* (Syracuse, NY: Syracuse University Press).

Douglas, M. and Wildavsky, A. (1982) *Risk and Culture: An Essay on the Selection of Technological and Environmental Dangers* (Berkeley: University of California Press).

Dreyfus, S.E. (1985) 'Beyond rationality', in M. Grauer, M. Thompson and A. Wierzbicki (eds), *Plural Rationality and Interactive Decision Processes*, Lecture Notes in Economics and Mathematical Systems No. 248 (Berlin: Springer), pp. 55–64.

Dror, Y. (1968) *Public Policy Re-examined* (Scranton, PA: Chandler).

Dror, Y. (1976) 'Some features of a meta-model for policy studies', in P. Gregg (ed), *Problems of Theory in Policy Analysis* (Lexington, MA: Lexington Books), pp. 247–55.

Easton, D. (1965) *A Framework for Political Analysis* (Englewood Cliffs, NJ: Prentice Hall).

Edelman, M. (1964) *The Symbolic Uses of Politics* (Urbana, IL: University of Illinois Press).

Edelman, M. (1971) *Politics as Symbolic Action: Mass Arousal and Quiescence* (Chicago: Markham).

Edelman, M. (1988) *Constructing the Political Spectacle* (Chicago: Chicago University Press).

Elder, C.D. and Cobb, R.W. (1983) *The Political Uses of Symbols* (London: Longman).

Elster, J. (1979) 'Risk, uncertainty and nuclear power', *Social Science Information*, 18: 371–400.

Etzioni, A. (1968) *The Active Society* (New York: Free Press).

Eva, D. and Rothman, H. (1979) Control of environmental impacts of technology, in P. Gummet and R. Johnston (eds) *Directing Technology: Policies for Promotion and Control* (London: Croom Helm) pp. 156–74.

Evans-Pritchard, E.E. (1937) *Witchcraft, Oracles and Magic Among the Azande* (Oxford: Clarendon Press).

Fallows, S. (1979) *The Nuclear Waste Disposal Controversy*, in Nelkin (1979), pp. 87–124.

Fischoff, B., Lichtenstein, S., Slovic, D., Derby, S.L. and Keeney, R. (1981) *Acceptable Risk* (Cambridge: Cambridge University Press).

Francis, A., Turk, J. and Willman, P. (eds) (1983) *Power, Efficiency and Institutions* (London: Heinemann Educational).

Frankena, F. (1983) 'Facts, values and technical expertise in a renewable energy siting dispute', *Journal of Economic Psychology*, 4: 131–47.

Garson, D.G. (1978) *Group Theories in Politics* (Beverly Hills; CA: Sage).

Geertz, C. (1973) *The Interpretation of Culture* (New York: Basic Books).

Georgescu-Roegen, N. (1974) *The Entropy Law and Economic Progress* (Cambridge, MA: Harvard University Press).

Gershuny, J.I. (1978) 'Policymaking rationality: A reformulation', *Policy Sciences*, 9: 295–316.

Gershuny, J.I. (1981) 'What should forecasters do? A pessimistic view', in P. Baehr and B. Wittrock (eds), *Policy Analysis and Policy Innovation — Patterns, Problems and Potentials* (London: Sage), pp. 193–207.

Gillespie, B., Eva, D. and Johnston, R. (1979) 'Carcinogenic risk assessment in the United States and Great Britain: The case of Aldrin/Dieldrin', *Social Studies of Science*, 9: 265–301.

Gilpin, R. (1962) *American Scientists and Nuclear Weapons Policy* (Princeton, NJ: Princeton University Press).

Goodman, N. (1978) *Ways of Worldmaking* (Indianapolis, ID: Hackett).

Grauer, M., Thompson, M. and Wierzbicki, A.P. (eds) (1985) *Plural Rationality and Interactive Decision Processes*, Lecture Notes in Economics and Mathematical Systems No. 248 (Berlin: Springer).

Gross, J. and Rayner, S. (1985) *Measuring Culture* (New York: Columbia University Press).

Hacking, I. (1975) *The Emergence of Probability: A Philosophical Study of Early Ideas About Probability, Induction and Statistical Inference* (Cambridge: Cambridge University Press).

Häfele, W. (1981) *Energy in a Finite World*, vol. 2 (Cambridge, MA: Ballinger).

Hapgood, F. (1979) 'Risk–benefit analysis: Putting a price on life', *The Atlantic*.

Harman, W.W., Reuyl, J.S., Carlson, R.C., Levine, M.D. and Witwer, J.G. (1977) *Solar Energy in America's Future, Second Edition*, (Stanford: Stanford University Research Institute).

Hetman, F. (1973) *Society and the Assessment of Technology* (Paris: OECD).

Hirschmann, A.O. and Lindblom, C.E. (1970) *Exit, Voice and Loyalty* (Cambridge, MA: Harvard University Press).

Hohenemser, C. and Kasperson, J.X. (1982) *Risk in the Technological Society*, (Boulder, CO: Westview Press).

Holling, C.S. (1979) 'Myths of ecological stability', in G. Smart and W. Stansbury (eds), *Studies in Crisis Management* (Montreal: Butterworth).

Holling, C.S. (1986) 'The resilience of terrestrial ecosystems', in W. Clark and R. Munn (eds), *Sustainable Development of the Biosphere* (Cambridge: Cambridge University Press).

Hughes, T.P. (1989) *American Genesis: A Century of Invention and Technological Enthusiasm* (New York: Viking).

Humphrey, C.R. and Buttel, F.H. (1980) 'The sociology of the growth/no growth debate', *Policy Studies*, 5: 336–45.

Irwin, A. (1985) *Risk and the Control of Technology: Public Policies for Road Traffic Safety in Britain and the United States* (Manchester: Manchester University Press).

Jenkins, W.I. (1978) *Policy Analysis: A Political and Organizational Perspective* (London: Martin Robertson).

Kahnemann, D. and Tversky, A. (1982) 'The psychology of preferences', *Scientific American*, Jan 1982, pp. 136–42.

Keepin, B., Wynne, B. and Thompson, M. (1984) 'The IIASA energy study', *Policy Sciences*, 17, No. 3, 197–339.

Keepin, B. and Wynne, B. (1984) Technical analysis of the IIASA energy scenarios', *Nature*, 312: 691–5.

Keynes, J.M. (1973) *Treatise on Probability* (London: Macmillan).

Knight, F.H. (1921) *Risk, Uncertainty and Profit* (republished 1965, Harper and Row).

Knorr-Cetina, K.D. and Mulkay, M. (eds) (1983) *Science Observed: Perspectives on the Social Study of Science* (London: Sage).

Kunreuther, H.C., Linnerooth, J., Lathrop, J., Atz, H., Macgill, S., Mandl, C., Schwarz, M. and Thompson, M. (1983) *Risk Analysis and Decision Processes: The Siting of Liquefied Energy Gas Facilities in Four Countries* (Berlin: Springer).

Lakatos, I. (1976) *Proofs and Refutations: the Logic of Mathematical Discovery* (Cambridge: Cambridge University Press).

La Porte, T.R. (ed) (1975) *Organized Social Complexity* (Princeton, NJ: Princeton University Press).

Lasswell, H. (1958) *Politics: Who Gets What, When and How?* (Cleveland: Meridian Books).

Law, J. and French, D. (1974) 'Normative and interpretive sociologies of science', *Sociological Review*, 31: 581–95.

Lawless, E.W. (1977) *Technology and Social Shock* (New Brunswick, NJ:

Rutgers University Press).

Lindblom, C.E. (1959) 'The science of muddling through', *Public Adminis-tration Review*, 39: 79–99.

Lindblom, C.E. (1965) *The Intelligence of Democracy* (New York: Free Press).

Lindblom, C.E. (1977) *Politics and Markets* (New York: Basic Books).

Lindblom, C.E. (1979) 'Still muddling, not yet through', *Public Administration Review*, 39: 517–626.

Lovins, A. (1977) *Soft Energy Paths* (Harmondsworth: Penguin).

Lowrance, W.W. (1976) *Of Acceptable Risk* (Los Altos, CA: William Kaufman).

Lyons, D. (1988) *The Information Society: Issues and Illusions* (Cambridge: Polity Press).

MacLean, D. (1982) 'Risk and consent: Philosophical issues for centralized decisions', *Risk Analysis*, 2: 59–67.

MacLean, D. (1986) 'Risk and consent: Philosophical issues for centralized decisions', in D. Maclean (ed), *Values at Risk* (Totowa, NJ: Rowman and Allanheld), pp. 17–30.

Majone, G. (1982) 'The uncertain logic of standard-setting', *Zeitschrift für Umweltpolitik*, 4: 317–29.

Majone, G. (1985) *The Uses of Policy Analysis* (New Haven, CT: Yale University Press).

March, J.G. and Olsen, J.P. (1976) *Ambiguity and Choice in Organisations* (Bergen: Universitetsforlaget).

March, J.G. and Simon, H.E. (1958) *Organizations* (New York: Wiley).

Mazur, A. (1973) 'Disputes between experts', *Minerva*, 11: 243–62.

Mazur, A. (1981) *The Dynamics of Technical Controversy* (Washington, DC: Communications Press).

Mazur, A., Marino, A.A. and Becker, R.O. (1979) 'Separating factual disputes from value disputes in controversies over technology', *Technology in Society*, 1: 229–37.

Morell, D. and Magorian, C. (1982) *Siting Hazardous Waste Facilities: Local Opposition and the Myth of Preemption* (Cambridge, MA: Ballinger).

Muir Wood, A.M. (1980) Letter to *The Times*, 7 February 1980.

Mulkay, M. (1979) *Science and the Sociology of Knowledge* (London: Allen and Unwin).

Nelkin, D. (1971) *Nuclear Power and its Critics: The Cayuga Lake Controversy*, (Ithaca: Cornell University Press).

Nelkin, D. (1974a) *Jetport: The Boston Airport Controversy* (New Brunswick, NJ: Transaction Books).

Nelkin, D. (1974b) 'The role of experts in a nuclear siting controversy', *Bulletin of the Atomic Scientists*, 30: 29–36.

Nelkin, D. (1975) 'The political impact of technical expertise', *Social Studies of Science*, 5: 35–54.

Nelkin, D. (1977) 'Technology and public policy', in I. Spiegel Rosing and D. de Solla Price (eds), *Science, Technology and Society: A Cross-disciplinary Perspective* (London: Sage), pp. 393–441.

Nelkin, D. (ed) (1979) *Controversy: Politics of Technical Decisions* (London: Sage).

Nelkin, D. (1983) 'On the social and political acceptability of risk', *Impact of Science on Society*, 4: 225–31.

Nelkin, D. and Pollak, M. (1982) *The Atom Besieged: Antinuclear Movements in France and Germany* (Cambridge, MA: MIT Press).

Newby, E. (1966) *Slowly Down the Ganges* (London: Picador).

Nichols, K.G. (1979) 'The de-institutionalization of technical expertise', in H. Skoie (ed), *Scientific Expertise and the Public* (Oslo, Institute for Studies in Research and Higher Education), pp. 35–48.

Nisbett, R.E. and Borgida, E. (1975) 'Attribution and the psychology of prediction', *Journal of Personal and Social Psychology*, 32: 923–43.

Nowotny, H. (1977) 'Scientific purity and nuclear danger', in E. Mendelsohn, P. Weingart and R. Whitley (eds), *The Social Production of Scientific Knowledge Sociology of the Sciences Yearbook 1977* (Dordrecht: Reidel), pp. 243–64.

Nowotny, H. (1979) *Kernenergie: Gefahr oder Notwendigkeit* (Frankfurt-am-Main: Suhrkamp).

Nowotny, H. (1980) 'The role of experts in developing public policy: The Austrian debate on nuclear power', *Science Technology and Human Values*, 5: 10–18.

O'Hare, M., Sanderson, D. and Bacow, L. (1983) *Facility Siting and Public Opposition* (New York: Van Nostrand).

Organisation for Economic Co-operation and Development (1978) *Social Assessment of Technology: A Review of Selected Case Studies* (Paris: OECD).

Organisation for Economic Co-operation and Development (1979) *Technology on Trial: Public Participation in Decision-making Related to Science and Technology* (Paris: OECD).

Orr, D.W. (1977) 'US energy policy and the political economy of participation', *Journal of Politics*, 41: 1027–56.

Ostrander, D. (1982) *One- and Two-dimensional Models of the Distribution of Beliefs*, in Douglas, M. (ed) (1982), pp. 14–30.

Ouchi, W.G. (1980) 'Markets, bureaucracies and clans', *Administrative Science Quarterly*, 25: 95–100.

Petersen, J.C. and Markle, G.E. (1979) 'Politics and science in the Laetrile controversy', *Social Studies of Science*, 9: 139–66.

Pfeffer, J. (1981) 'Management as symbolic action', in L.L. Cummings and B.M. Staw (eds), *Research in Organizational Behaviour*, vol. 3 (Greenwich, CT: JAI Press), pp. 339–441.

Porter, A.L. *et al.* (1982) *A Guidebook for Technology Assessment* (Lexington, MA: D.C. Heath).

Pye, L.W. (1973) 'Culture and political science: Problems in the evaluation of the concept of political culture', in L. Schneider and C.M. Bonjean (eds), *The Idea of Culture in the Social Sciences* (Cambridge: Cambridge University Press).

Rasmussen, N.C. *et al.* (1975) *Reactor Safety Study, WASH 1400*, US Nuclear Regulatory Commission (NUREG-75/014).

Rayner, S. (1984) 'Disagreeing about risk', in S. Hadden (ed) *Risk Analysis, Institutions and Public Policy* (New York: Associated Faculty Press).

Rayner, S. (1986) 'Management of radiation hazards in hospitals: Plural rationalities in a single institution', *Social Studies of Science*, 16: 573–91.

Rayner, S. and Cantor, R. (1987) 'How fair is safe enough? The cultural approach to societal technology choice', *Risk Analysis*, 7: 3–9.

Riley, P. (1983) 'A structurationist account of political culture', *Administrative Science Quarterly*, 28: 414–37.

Rip, A. (1983) *Comparative Study of Science-Related Controversies: Avoiding Blind Spots.* (Discussion paper presented at the 4th Annual Meeting, 4–6 November, 1983, Blacksburg, Virginia).

Rip, A. (1984) *Controversies as Informal Technology Assessment*, Science and Technology Studies Program, University of Leiden.

Rip, A. and van den Belt, H. (1986) 'Constructive technology assessment: Influencing technological development?', *Journal für Entwicklungspolitik*, 3: 24–40.

Robbins, D. and Johnston R. (1976) 'The role of cognitive and occupational differentiation in scientific controversies', *Social Studies of Science*, 6: 349–68.

Roessner, D.J. and Frey, J. (1974) 'Methodology for technology assessment', *Technological Forecasting and Social Change*, 6: 163–9.

Rothschild, Lord (1978) 'Risk', *The Listener*, 30 November 1978.

Rothschild-Whitt, J. (1979) 'The collectivist organization: An alternative to rational-bureacratic models', *American Sociological Review*, 14: 509–27.

Schanz, J.J. Jr (1978) 'Oil and gas resources: welcome to uncertainty', *Resources*, 58, special issue, March 1978.

Schattschneider, E.E. (1960) *The Semisovereign People* (New York: Holt, Rinehart and Winston).

Schmutzer, M.E.A. and Bandler, W. (1980) 'Hi and Low, in and out: Approaches to social status', *Cybernetics* 10: 289–99.

Schooler, D. (1971) *Science, Scientists and Public Policy* (New York: Free Press).

Schulze, W.D. (1980) 'Ethics, economics and the value of safety', in R.C. Schwing and W.A. Albers (eds) *Societal Risk Assessment* (New York: Plenum), pp. 217–31.

Schumacher, E.F. (1973) *Small is Beautiful* (London: Blond and Briggs).

Schwarz, M. (1983) 'Controversial decision-making: LNG technology in the Netherlands' in Umweltbundesamt (hrsg), 119–34.

Segal, H.P. (1982) 'Assessing retrospective technology assessment', *Technology in Society*, 4: 231–46.

Sheehan, S. (1975) *A Welfare Mother* (New York: New American Library).

Silcock, B. (1979) 'Risky business', in *The Sunday Times*, (30 December)

Simon, H.A. (1947) *Administrative Behaviour* (New York: Macmillan); 2nd edn 1957.

Simon, H.A. (1955) 'A behavioural model of rational choice', *Quarterly Journal of Economics* 99: 99–118.

Simon, H.A. (1976) 'From substantive to procedural rationality', in S.J. Latsis (ed.) *Method and Appraisal in Economics* (Cambridge: Cambridge University Press).

Slovic, P., Fischoff, B. and Lichtenstein, S. (1976) 'Cognitive processes and societal risk taking', in J.S. Carroll and J.W. Payne (eds), *Cognition and Social Behaviour* (Hillsdale, NJ: Erlbaum).

Slovic, P., Fishoff, B. and Lichtenstein, S. (1979) 'Which risks are acceptable?', *Environment*, 21, No. 4.

Smircich, L. (1983) 'Concepts of culture and organisational analysis', *Administrative Science Quarterly*, 28: 339–58.

Smith, G. and May, D. (1980) 'The artificial debate', *Policy and Politics*, 3: 147–61.

Smits, R.E.H.M.; Leyten, A.J.M. and Geurts, J.L.A. (1987) 'The possibilities and limitations of technology assessment: In search of a useful approach', *Technology Assessment: An Opportunity for Europe* vol. 1 (The Hague: Dutch Ministry of Education and Science/Commission of the European Communities/FAST).

Spronk, J., and Veeneklass, F. (1983) 'A feasibility study of economic and environmental scenarios by means of interactive multiple goal programming', *Regional Science and Urban Economics*, 13: 141–60.

Thompson, H.S. (1980) *The Great Shark Hunt* (London: Picador/Pan).

Thompson, M. (1978) 'Out with the boys again', in K. Wilson (ed) *The Games Climbers Play* (London: Diadem).

Thompson, M. (1979) *Rubbish Theory: The Creation and Destruction of Value* (Oxford: Oxford University Presss).

Thompson, M. (1982a) *Among the Energy Tribes: The Anthropology of the Current Policy Debate*, Working Paper WP-82-59 (Laxenburg, Austria, International Institute for Applied Systems Analysis).

Thompson, M. (1982b) *A Three-Dimensional Model*, in M. Douglas (ed) (1982a), pp. 31–63.

Thompson, M. (1982c) 'The problem of the centre: An autonomous cosmology', in M. Douglas (ed), *Essays in the Sociology of Perception* (London, Routledge and Kegan Paul), pp. 302–38.

Thompson, M. (1983a) *Postscript: A Cultural Basis for Comparison*, in H.C. Kunreuther, J. Linnerooth, *et al.*, *Risk Analysis and Decision Processes* (Berlin: Springer).

Thompson, M. (1983b) 'The aesthetics of risk: Culture or context?', in R. Schwing and W. Albers (eds), *Societal Risk Assessment* (New York: Plenum).

Thompson, M. (1986) 'To hell with turkeys: A diatribe directed at the pernicious trepidity of the current intellectual debate on risk', in D. MacLean (ed) *Values at Risk* (Totowa, NJ: Rowan and Allanheld), pp. 113–35.

Thompson, M. (1987) 'Welche Gesellschaftsklassen sind potent genug, anderen ihre Zukunft aufzuoktroyieren? Und wie geht das vor sich?', in L. Burchardt (ed) *Design der Zukunft* (Berlin: Dumont/International Design Centre), pp. 58–87.

Thompson, M. (1988) 'Socially viable ideas of nature: A cultural hypothesis', in E. Baark and U. Svedin (eds) *Man, Nature and Technology: Essays on the Role of Ideological Perceptions* (London: Macmillan), pp. 80–104.

Thompson, M. and Warburton, M. (1985) 'Decision-making under contradictory certainties: How to save the Himalayas when you can't find out what is wrong with them', *Journal of Applied Systems Analysis*, 12: 3–34.

Thompson, M. and Tayler, P. (1986) 'The surprise game: An exploration of constrained relativism', *Warwick Papers in Management*, 1 (Institute for Management Research and Development, University of Warwick).

Thompson, M., Warburton, M. and Hatley, T. (1986) *Uncertainty on a Himalayan Scale* (London: Ethnographica).

Thompson, M. and Wildavsky, A. (1986a) 'A cultural theory of information bias in organisations', *Journal of Management Studies*, 23(3): 273–86.

Thompson, M. and Wildavsky, A. (1986b) 'A poverty of distinction: From economic homogeneity to cultural heterogeneity in the classification of poor people', *Policy Sciences*, 19: 163–99.

Timmerman, P. (1986) 'Myths and paradigms of interactions between development and environment', in W.C. Clark and R.E. Munn (eds) *Sustainable Development of the Biosphere* (Cambridge: Cambridge University Press).

TNO (1984) *Technology Assessment: Op zoek naar een bruikbare aanpak. Rapport 1. Analyse van de mogelijkheden en beperkingen* (Den Haag: Staatsuitgeverij).

Tribe, L. (1973) 'Technology assessment and the fourth discontinuity: The limits of instrumental rationality', *Southern California Law Review*, 46: 617–60.

Tribe, L.H. (1976) 'Ways not to think about plastic trees', in L.H. Tribe, C.S. Schelling and J. Vos (eds) *When Values Conflict: Essays on Environmental Analysis, Discourse and Decision* (Cambridge, MA: Ballinger), pp. 61–91.

Turney, J. and Schwarz, M. (1983) 'Holland's great debate on energy', *Town and Country Planning* 52: 79–81.

Umweltbundesamt (hrsg) (1983) *Technologien auf dem Prüfstand – Die Rolle der Technologiefolgenabschatzung im Entscheidungsprozess* (Köln: Carl Heymanns Verlag).

Ward, C. (1987) 'Risk and uncertainty', *New Society*, 6.

Weber, M. (1958) *The Protestant Ethic and the Spirit of Capitalism* (New York: Free Press).

Weinberg, A. (1972) 'Science and trans-science', *Minerva*, 10: 209–22.

Wenk, E. (1984) 'Civic competence to manage technology', *Technological Forecasting and Social Change*, 26: 127–33.

Whillans, D. (1984) As reported on the occasion of Whillans' fiftieth birthday by Ronald Faux in an article 'The Only Way is up', *The Times*, 26 March.

Whitehead, A.N. (1926) *Science and the Modern World* (New York: Macmillan).

Wildavsky, A. (1982) 'The three cultures: Explaining anomalies in the American welfare state', *Public Interest*, Fall, pp. 45–58.

Wildavsky, A. (1988) *Searching for Safety* (New Brunswick/Oxford: Social Philosophy and Policy Centre/Transaction Publishers).

Wildavsky, A. and Tenenbaum, E. (1981) *The Politics of Mistrust: Estimating American Oil and Gas Reserves* (Beverly Hills, CA: Sage).

Williamson, O.E. (1973) 'Markets and hierarchies: Some elementary considerations', *American Economic Review*, 63: 316–25.

Williamson, O. (1975) *Markets and Hierarchies* (New York: Free Press).

Williamson, O.E. and Ouchi, W.G. (1983) 'The markets and hierarchies programme of research: Origins, implications, prospects', in A. Francis, J. Turk and P. Willman (eds) (1983), pp. 13–34.

Winner, L. (1977) *Autonomous Technology: Technics-out-of-control as a Theme in Political Thought* (Cambridge, MA: MIT Press).

Winner, L. (1980) 'Do artefacts have politics?', *Daedalus*, 109: 121–36.

Wynne, B. (1974) 'The rhetoric of consensus politics: A critical review of technology assessment', *Research Policy*, 5: 1–56.

Wynne, B. (1980) 'Technology, risk, and participation: On the social treatment of uncertainty', in J. Conrad (ed) (1980), pp. 173–208.

Wynne, B. (1982a) 'Institutional mythologies and dual societies in the management of risk', in H.C. Kunreuther and E.V. Ley (eds) *The Risk Analysis Controversy: An Institutional Perspective* (Berlin: Springer).

Wynne B. (1982b) *Rationality and Ritual: The Windscale Inquiry and Nuclear Decisions in Britain* (Chalfont St Giles, Bucks: Society for the History of Science).

Wynne, B. (1983) 'Redefining the issues of risk and acceptance: The social viability of technology', *Futures*, 15: 13–32.

Wynne, B. (1984) *Risk Assessment of Technological Systems: Dimensions of Uncertainty*, Working Paper WP-84-42 (Laxenburg, Austria: International Institute for Applied Systems Analysis).

Wynne, B. (1985) 'Review of *Social Constraints on Technological Progress* by R. Coppock; *Political Quarterly*, 56: 315–17.

Wynne, B. (1987) *Risk Management and Hazardous Waste: Implementation and the Dialectics of Credibility* (London: Springer).

Wynne, B. (1989) 'Frameworks of rationality in risk management: Towards the testing of naive sociology', in J. Brown (ed) *Environmental Threats: Perception, Analysis and Management* (London: Belhaven).

Wynne, B. and Otway, H.J. (1982) 'Information technology, power and managers', in N. Bjorn-Anderson, *et al.* (eds) *Information Society: For Richer for Poorer* (Amsterdam: North Holland).

Young, O.R. (1968) *Systems of Political Science* (Englewood Cliffs, NJ: Prentice Hall).

Index